Gender, Migration and Remittances in Southern Africa

Belinda Dodson with Hamilton Simelane,
Daniel Tevera, Thuso Green, Abel Chikanda
and Fion de Vletter

Series Editor:
Prof. Jonathan Crush

Southern African Migration Project
2008

Editorial Note

This report is the third in an ongoing series using SAMP's extensive MARS data base which provides detailed information on the volume, channels, impacts and development potential of remittances in the SADC (see Nos. 43 and 44). SAMP wishes to thank Bruce Frayne, Wade Pendleton and Krista House for their management of the MARS project and Christa Schier for her work on the data base. The country research teams were led by Hamilton Simelane (Swaziland), Daniel Tevera and Abel Chikanda (Zimbabwe), Thuso Green (Lesotho), Fion de Vletter (Mozambique), Maxton Tsoka (Malawi) and Eugene Campbell and K.T.O. Balogi (Botswana). SAMP is particularly grateful to Belinda Dodson for agreeing to conduct a gender analysis of the MARS data. MARS and this report were funded by the UK Department for International Development (DFID).

Published by Idasa, 6 Spin Street, Church Square, Cape Town, 8001, and Southern African Research Centre, Queen's University, Canada.

Copyright Southern African Migration Project (SAMP) 2008
ISBN 978-1-920118-70-9

First published 2008
Design by Bronwen Müller
Typeset in Goudy

CONTENTS   PAGE

TABLES   PAGE

EXECUTIVE SUMMARY

Migrant remittances have become an important source of income for many developing countries, exceeding official development assistance. As a result, migration and remittance behaviour are becoming a growing focus of international attention. Understanding the processes and patterns of remittance behaviour can help shed light on their usage and impact, both on recipient households and on wider socio-economic development in migrant-origin countries. One key aspect of such an understanding is the gender dynamics of migration and remittance practices. Globally, there is evidence of the feminization of migrant flows, with women increasingly migrating as independent migrants in their own right. Female migrants maintain strong ties to family members in their home countries. These include significant flows of remittances, of both cash and goods, sent to family members at home.

Southern Africa has a long history of cross-border migration and associated flows of remittances. Although cross-border economic migration in the region has been dominated by male migrant labour to the South African mining industry, women have also engaged in movement across the region's borders for purposes of seeking work. Evidence suggests that female migration in the region, especially to South Africa, has increased significantly over the past 10-15 years. Little is known about the nature of migrant women's remittances and their impact on the households that receive them, nor about the changing patterns of male and female migration over the past decade.

SAMP devised the Migration and Remittances Surveys (MARS) to provide nationally-representative data on remittance flows and usage at the household level for five SADC countries: Botswana, Lesotho, Mozambique, Swaziland and Zimbabwe. SAMP-led research teams in each country conducted the survey using a standardized questionnaire and sampling strategy. Households were randomly selected and included in the survey only if they had members who were cross-border migrants working outside the country.

The MARS survey collected two different types of data: data on individual household members, both migrant and non-migrant, and data on migrant-sending households. In total, 4,700 household interviews were conducted in the five countries and information collected on over 30,000 people. In addition to questions about migrant destinations, occupations and demographics, questions were asked about remittance behaviour, the methods used for remittance transfer, the role of remittances in the migrant-sending household economy, and the impact of migrant remittances on migrant-sending households. Gender-related variables were included in the survey through a question asking the sex of individual household members, and also in terms of household headship, marital status, relationship to the head of household, and household type (e.g. female- or male-centered; nuclear or extended).

The overall survey findings have been presented in an earlier SAMP report (Migration Policy Series No. 44). Building on that earlier report, this report presents a gender breakdown and analysis of the MARS findings. As the Botswana sample included only a very small number of female migrants, Botswana has been left out of the analysis and so the report covers the four countries of Lesotho, Mozambique, Swaziland and Zimbabwe. Gender analysis reveals significant gender-based differences in migrant demographics, including divergent patterns and trends between male and female migrants in terms of their age and marital status. Yet it also reveals striking similarities between male and female migrants in terms of the nature, role and impact of their remittances.

The main findings in terms of migrant demographics and migration trends for men and women are as follows:

- Cross-border migration in the region remains dominated by men. Overall, just over 15% of the migrants identified in the MARS sample were women. The proportion of women amongst migrants varies widely from country to country. Zimbabwe stands out as the country with by far the highest proportion of migrants who are female, at 43.6%, with Lesotho a distant second at 16.4%. In the other countries surveyed, the proportion of migrants who are female was found to be below 10%.

- Although the lack of reliable benchmark data makes it impossible to quantify, the MARS data suggests that there has been an increase in female migration over the period 1994-2004. Compared to female migrants, a relatively higher proportion of male migrants had been migrating for periods of over a decade - except in the case of Zimbabwe, where extensive out-migration is a more recent phenomenon for both men and women.

- The type of women who migrate appears to have undergone significant changes. Migration surveys conducted by SAMP in the late 1990s showed that female migrants were more likely to be older and to be married than male cross-border migrants. MARS findings show that today's female migrants are younger and less likely to be married than male migrants.

- The proportion of female migrants in the younger, 15-24 age bracket is significantly higher than the equivalent proportion for males in Lesotho, Mozambique and Swaziland. In these same three countries, men are correspondingly over-represented in the older, 40-59 age bracket compared to women. Zimbabwean male and female migrants' age profiles were roughly equivalent, with the majority in the 25-39 age bracket.

- In all four countries, and especially in Mozambique and Swaziland, the category containing the highest proportion of female migrants was 'daughter' – almost three-quarters of the female migrants in Mozambique and two-thirds in Swaziland. These countries' female migrants thus most closely conform to the historical pattern of migration to South Africa being dominated by young, unmarried adults.
- On the male side of the equation, migration appears to be increasing among older, married heads of household. Some 76% of male migrants from Lesotho and 61% of those from Swaziland are heads of their household. Male migration from Mozambique is still dominated by sons (49%); that from Zimbabwe is more or less equally divided between sons and household heads. This suggests that for men, migration is becoming a career path rather than just a temporary phenomenon at a particular stage in younger men's lives, whereas young single women are engaging in migration practices traditionally found amongst young single men.
- In Lesotho, Mozambique and Zimbabwe, female migrants revealed higher levels of divorce, separation, abandonment and widowhood than their male counterparts. This is especially true of Lesotho, where 24% of female migrants are widows and a further 20% divorced or separated. These women are likely to be the primary or sole breadwinner for their families.
- Female migration and female household headship appear to be closely linked. Among female migrants, the proportion coming from female-centred households, having no husband or male partner, was 43% for Lesotho, 41% for Mozambique, 31% for Swaziland and 28% for Zimbabwe. In addition, 24% of the female migrants from Lesotho and 17% of those from Zimbabwe, the two countries with the highest proportions of women among their migrants, were themselves household heads. Male migrants hail predominantly from male-headed, nuclear or extended-family households.
- Female migrants from Lesotho and Swaziland are better educated than male migrants. Men from these countries are over-represented in the categories of 'none' or 'primary' education, while women migrants are more likely than men to have some secondary schooling. Mozambique has the least educated migrants of the four countries, with close to three quarters of both male and female migrants having only primary education. Zimbabwean male and female migrants have roughly equivalent education pro-

files, with a highly educated migrant cohort in which over 75% have secondary education or above.

The geographical and economic profiles of male and female migration also display both similarities and divergences. Here, the main findings are as follows:

- For both male and female migrants, the main destination is South Africa. Lesotho's migration is almost entirely (99%) to South Africa, as is that of Swazi men. Some women migrants from Swaziland can be found working in countries beyond the region (13.5%). Mozambique sends small numbers of migrants, especially women, to Swaziland, Botswana and other SADC countries in addition to South Africa. Zimbabwe is again the exception, with only one third of its migrants (male and female) in South Africa and 40% working in countries beyond Southern Africa.

- Perhaps the greatest difference between male and female migrants is in their activity and employment profiles. Minework is still the predominant form of employment for male migrants from Lesotho, Swaziland and Mozambique. Almost 80% of male migrants from Lesotho and two-thirds from Swaziland work on the South African mines. In the case of Mozambique, the figure is one-third. Male migrants from Mozambique also work in a range of non-mining occupations including skilled and unskilled manual labour (18%). Zimbabwe's more educated male migrants work in professional and service occupations, while others are engaged in trade. Few men from the other three countries listed trade as an occupation.

- In general, women migrants are spread across a wider range of occupations than their male counterparts. Relative to male migrants, female migrants are less likely to be in formal employment and more likely to be engaged in informal economic activity. Trading is a significant economic activity for female migrants from all four countries, with trade being particularly important as an occupation for women from Mozambique and Zimbabwe. Domestic service is a more significant form of employment for women from Lesotho and Swaziland. Informal sector production is another important occupation for female migrants. Agricultural, manual and 'other service' work occupy a small but significant number of migrant women. Among more skilled women, professional and office occupations are common, and 16% of Zimbabwe's female migrants are employed in the health sector.

Given this gender difference in occupation and employment, any similarities or differences between men and women in their remittance practices, and in the extent to which their households depend on those remittances, are of interest. The MARS findings outlined below demonstrate the extent and significance of remittance income to recipient households.

- For most migrant-sending households, migrant remittances form the main source of household income, although male migrants' remittances are more likely to be the primary or sole source of income for their households. Lesotho has the highest incidence of households reporting remittance earnings, followed by Zimbabwe, Mozambique and Swaziland. Households reporting remittance income from male and female migrants respectively in each of the four countries was: Lesotho 96% (M) and 90% (F); Zimbabwe 85% (M) and 78% (F); Mozambique 77% (M) and 65% (F); and Swaziland 63% (M) and 64% (F).

- The amounts of money remitted by female migrants are significantly lower than those of male migrants, in part reflecting women migrants' lower levels of income and employment security. Gender differences are most stark in Mozambique and Lesotho. Zimbabwe's more gender-equivalent migration profile is again borne out in the remittance data, with men and women remitting similar amounts. The median annual values of remittances received by male migrant-sending households were: R9,600 in Lesotho; R2,011 in Mozambique; R2,400 in Swaziland; and R1,093 in Zimbabwe. For households sending female migrants, median remittance receipts were: R3,600 in Lesotho; R302 in Mozambique; R1,800 in Swaziland; and R1,093 in Zimbabwe.

- Despite remitting less than men, Lesotho's female migrants still remit larger sums than female migrants from any of the other three countries: twice as much as second-placed Swaziland, three times as much as women from Zimbabwe, and ten times as much as women from Mozambique. This probably reflects the higher incidence of household headship among Lesotho's women migrants, possibly along with higher earnings than women from other countries (e.g. as domestic workers rather than informal traders).

- Lesotho's migrant-sending households displayed the highest dependence on remittance earnings, reporting fewer alternative sources of income. By contrast, many households in the other three countries had remittances as part of a bundle of income-earning strategies, including wage work, casual work and formal or informal business, although remittances remain their primary source of income. Multiple sources of income were found especially among households sending female migrants. Female migrants remit lower sums, making other household income sources a necessity. Women are also less likely than men to be household heads, which means that they are often members of households with other working adult members.

- The proportion of female migrants sending home goods is slightly higher than the equivalent proportion of male migrants, especially in Zimbabwe (72% of women, 62% of men) and to a lesser extent Lesotho (23% of women, 20% of men). In Mozambique and Swaziland, male and female migrants were equally likely to remit goods, at 65% and 16% respectively. Zimbabwe and Mozambique had the highest incidence of non-monetary remittances, whereas monetary remittances were much more significant in Lesotho and Swaziland.

The significance and impact of both male and female migrants' remittances is evident in the contribution of remittances to household expenditure and the stated importance of remittances by recipient households:

- Household expenditure data show that the main household purchases for both male and female migrant-sending households are the basic commodities of food, domestic fuel and clothing, and fundamental services such as schooling, health care and transport.
- While the rank order of items purchased is broadly similar or even identical for male and female migrant-sending households, gender differences emerge in the actual proportion of households reporting a particular expenditure. In Lesotho, in almost every category, expenditure in the past month was reported by more male than female-migrant households. Gender-based patterns are more mixed in Mozambique, although lower proportions of female migrant-sending households reported expenditure in the key categories of food, clothing, medical expenses, education and transport. In Swaziland, there is no clear or consistent overall difference based on migrant gender. Zimbabwe displays the strongest similarity between expenditure in male and in female migrant-sending households, consistent with findings from the rest of the survey in that country. Certainly in Lesotho and Mozambique, female migrant-sending households do thus appear to be poorer than male migrant-sending households.
- There are also important gender differences, as well as differences between countries, in the estimated amounts of monthly expenditure on particular categories of expenses. Women migrants from Lesotho and Mozambique come from households with lower monthly expenditures, in almost every category, than households

with male migrants. Swaziland displays the opposite gender pattern. Swazi households where the migrant members are female spend more in each category than households with male migrant members. Zimbabwe again stands out as the country with strongest gender similarity, suggesting that its male and female migrants come from similar sorts of households in socio-economic terms.

- As the primary source of income for the majority of households, remittance earnings are vital in enabling households to meet their basic needs. Food is the most common annual expenditure of remittance money in all four countries and in both male and female migrant-sending households. Second in all countries is either clothing or school fees. Clothing or school fees also rank third in all countries except Swaziland, where purchases of agricultural inputs rank above clothing. Remittances do not appear to be spent on non-essential or luxury items; but nor are they commonly directed towards savings or investment in business or other productive activities. They are, however, significant in sources of investment in children's education.

- Remittance-receiving households confirmed the significance of remittances to food purchases. The most consistent importance rating, across countries and migrant genders, is food, with school fees and clothes also rated highly by many. There are some gender differences, with men's remittances seemingly more crucial to the purchase of basic livelihood items such as food, than women's. Given that men are older, more likely to be married, and more often the heads of households than female migrants, it is perhaps surprising that this gender difference is not greater.

- Remittances of goods are also focused on basic household commodities. The 'typical' male or female migrant sends home money, which their households use to buy food and other basic goods and services, and brings home clothing, food and other goods. Some consumer goods and other 'luxury' items (e.g. electronic goods) are also sent home, as they are more readily available and cheaper in South Africa.

- In addition to making regular remittances, migrants send home money in times of need, or to meet unexpected costs (such as funerals). Some gender differences are evident in these emergency remittances, although this is not consistent across all four countries. In Lesotho and Mozambique, a higher proportion of male migrants send money in times of need, whereas in Swaziland female migrants are more likely to do so. In Zimbabwe, once again, there is very little difference based on the gender of the migrant.

- Emergency remittances are clearly important to the households receiving them. They are seen as important or very important by over 90% of migrant-sending households in each of the four countries, with only very small differences on the basis of migrant gender. Emergency remittances appear to be especially significant to households in Swaziland and Zimbabwe.

Perceptions of the overall impact of migration reinforce the overall positive contribution made by migrants:

- There is a generally favourable view of cross-border migration. Respondents in Zimbabwe are the most positive. Close to 90% regard the impact of migration as either positive or very positive, with only a small difference based on the gender of the migrant. Respondents in the other three countries were broadly positive, although more so for male than for female migration. Close to 70% of the male migrant-sending household respondents in Lesotho, Mozambique and Swaziland regard migration as having positive or very positive impacts. The respective values for each country's female migrant-sending households were 59%, 53% and 64%.
- Perceptions of the positive impacts of working in another country reinforce the findings from income, expenditure and deprivation data i.e. that migrants support their households, improve living conditions and provide household income. Female migration is seen as providing the same sorts of benefits as male migration.
- While the economic benefits of migration are recognized, so too are some of its personal and social costs. These include loneliness, being away too long, and placing too much responsibility on family members left behind. The broad patterns are the same, irrespective of whether the migrant is male or female.

Remittances clearly play a vital role in supporting Southern African households. Not only do migrants, whether male or female, demonstrate an unusually high tendency to send money home to their families, but those remittances are fundamental in enabling families to meet their everyday needs. Remittance behaviour and the role of remittances in the household economy differ only slightly based on the gender of the migrant. This demonstrates that women's migration, while lower in volume than male migration, is nevertheless highly important to the migrant-sending household. Given that so many female migrants come from female-centred households, with no husband or male partner, women's migration is especially significant to such households as the primary – often only – source of household income.

The MARS data also suggest that differences between male and female migration, and between male and female migrants, are starting to diminish. Certainly young, unmarried women appear to be engaging in 'economic' migration more than they did previously, while male migration is extending into broader spheres of economic activity, both formal and informal, as well as into older age cohorts. If the patterns and trends identified here are both valid and sustained, women's cross-border migration in the region looks set to increase in extent and socio-economic significance.

INTRODUCTION

The feminization of migration is increasingly common in many parts of the world.[1] Women are migrating in greater numbers and not merely as dependants or trailing spouses, but as independent migrants in their own right. They generally still maintain close ties to family members left behind in their countries of origin. In Southern Africa, women have at no time been entirely absent from cross-border migrant flows.[2] While still in the minority relative to male migrants, they are today becoming a significant component of contemporary migration in the region. The volume of women's migration is increasing and re-shaping the overall economic and social impact of migration.[3]

Parallel to these changes in the gendering of international migration flows is a growing global recognition of the scale and significance of migrant remittances.[4] Cross-border migrants maintain personal, social and economic links that straddle international borders in various forms of transnational relationship and activity.[5] These include significant flows of both money and goods in what Guarnizo calls the 'economics of transnational living', with potentially significant implications for both sending and receiving countries.[6] A strong debate has emerged about the role of migrant remittances as a catalyst for socio-economic development in poor, migrant-sending countries, including countries in Africa.[7] Southern Africa presents an interesting case study as a well-established example of migrant remittances within the developing world (so called South-South remittances).[8] Migrant remittances are a long-standing practice in Southern Africa, playing an important historical and contemporary role in household and national economies. Historically, most remittances were sent home by male migrants. With the recent feminization of migration flows in the region, it is important to understand if male and female migrants display similar remittance behaviours. More generally, policymakers seeking to optimize the development value of remittances need to know how gender impacts on remittance volumes, dynamics, channels and uses.

SAMP has been systematically studying the relationship between migration, remittances and development in Southern Africa for several years. Given the paucity of data on the subject, a multi-country research initiative (the Migration and Remittances Survey or MARS) was launched in 2003. MARS was implemented in a number of key migrant origin countries in the SADC region in 2004-5: Botswana, Lesotho, Malawi, Mozambique, Swaziland and Zimbabwe. The first MARS report documented the general nature, role and significance of contemporary migrant remittances in Southern Africa.[9] Most remittances are from migrants going to relatively-prosperous South Africa from neighbouring countries. The study re-emphasizes the importance of migrant remittances to household livelihoods in this region, simultaneously signalling some of the important changes that have occurred in both migration processes and remittance practices in recent years.

While that analysis demonstrates the persistence of male dominance in regional cross-border migration, a gender breakdown of the data is warranted. The present report, based on the same data set, adds a gender lens to the analysis and understanding of migration and remittances in Southern Africa. The paper examines the role of gender as a factor in cross-border migration and remittance behaviour in Southern Africa.

SAMP MIGRATION AND REMITTANCES SURVEYS (MARS)

MARS was developed and implemented collaboratively by SAMP partners in a number of SADC countries. A standardized questionnaire and protocols for sampling as well as all other aspects of data collection and processing were developed. In addition to questions about migrant destinations, occupations and demographics, questions were asked about remittance behaviour, the methods used for remittance transfer, the role of remittances in the migrant-sending household economy, and the impact of migrant remittances on migrant-sending households.

These were national-scale surveys, with households first being randomly selected and then included in the survey if they answered "yes" to the question: 'Are there migrants who work outside this country living in this household?' A total of 4,700 households were identified in the sample. Data was collected on household attributes as well as the characteristics of individual household members, both migrants and non-migrants. This yielded a wealth of information on more than 30,000 people.

Only migrant-sending, and thus remittance-receiving, households were included in the sample. Migrants living 'away' in South Africa (or other countries) were not themselves interviewed. Further, the households captured in the MARS data set were those reporting members working outside the country, and thus excluded either migrants who were not working or migrants who had not left household members behind in their home countries. The data thus reflects the situation for economic migrants: people who live away from home for reasons related to their employment or occupation.

Gender-related variables were included in the survey through a question asking the sex of individual household members, and also in terms of household headship, marital status, relationship to the head of household, and household type (e.g. female- or male-centered; nuclear or extended). Cross-tabulating migrant sex with other variables and then comparing, first, male migrants to female migrants and, second, house-holds sending male migrants to households sending female migrants, allows a gender analysis of the survey findings. The analysis reveals significant gender-based differences in migrant demographics, but striking similarities between male and female migrants in terms of the nature, role and impact of their remittances.

In addition to drawing gender-based comparisons, this report presents an analysis broken down by country. Significant differences in migration and remittance behaviour amongst the countries surveyed have already been noted and discussed.[10] However, these differences also include gender-based variations. The gender analysis presented here therefore provides insights into the differences between countries in terms of overall migration and remittance behaviour. Zimbabwe stands out as the country with by far the highest proportion of migrants who are female, at 43.6%, with Lesotho a distant second at 16.4%. In each of the other three countries surveyed, the proportion of migrants who are female was found to be below 10%. The total number of female migrants in the Botswana sample was so low that it has been left out of this analysis. The findings presented here thus focus on the countries of Lesotho, Mozambique, Swaziland and Zimbabwe.

MARS has already facilitated a detailed account of the importance of migrant remittances to many households in South Africa's adjoining states.[11] The vast majority of migrant-sending households in the countries surveyed reported receiving cash remittances. These are a significant source of household income – on average equalling or exceeding any other single income source for those households having migrant members. The most common expenditure of remittance money was not on luxury consumer goods but on essentials such as food and clothing, along with items like school fees, house-building and transport. The picture is the same for goods remitted, with clothing and food, along with building materials, being the most common items sent. Migration is thus primarily a household livelihood strategy, critical for poverty alleviation and household subsistence, without necessarily having any broader developmental impact.

These observations regarding remittance behaviour are mirrored in the survey findings on the socio-demographic make-up of migrant streams from these countries. 'A few decades ago, sons and some daughters would have made up virtually all the migrant stream. Migration is now clearly a career rather than a passing phase in most people's working lives.'[12] Cross-border migration 'has become a livelihood strategy of the middle-aged', with only 7% of migrants being under 24 and 41% over 40.[13] Overall, most migrants are married heads of households rather than adult children or other household members. Precise earlier data on the extent of female migration is lacking, making it impossible to iden-tify clear trends, but the survey findings and other evidence suggest an increased incidence of female migration. For example, the majority of today's female migrants have been migrating for less than 10 years, in contrast to male migrants whose migration careers are generally of much longer duration.

Gender analysis of the MARS data provides important additional insight to this contemporary remittance picture. Earlier SAMP surveys, conducted in the late 1990s, revealed a number of interesting differences between men and women in regional practices of cross-border migra-tion.[14] Women migrants tended to stay in South Africa for shorter time periods, in a variety of circular, repeat, or relay forms of cross-border movement. Their major activities included legal and illegal employment as well as informal trade or 'shopping', while men's migration was more tied to formal labour migration, especially on the mines.[15] Do these gender differences persist, and do they extend to migrant remittances and their impact? If so, what are the implications, not only for female migrants and their family members, but also for livelihood strategies, pov-erty alleviation and economic development in the wider region?

PROFILING MALE AND FEMALE MIGRANTS

SAMP has already noted that the MARS data suggest a shift in the demographics of regional cross-border migration.[16] There has been an apparent ageing of the migrant population in general, along with an increased proportion of married heads of house-hold from the earlier prevalence of unmarried sons (and some daugh-ters). In migration surveys conducted by SAMP in the late 1990s, female migrants were found to be older, more likely to be married, and generally better educated than male cross-border migrants.[17] Are these differences in the demographic profile of migrant men and migrant women chang-ing? To answer this question, this section of the paper compares various socio-demographic attributes of male and female migrants from four countries surveyed in MARS. In addition to the overall sex breakdown of migrants, which reveals significant inter-country differences, data are presented on the relationship of migrants to the head of household along with their age, marital status and education status.

Table 1 shows the gender breakdown of the sample of migrants in each country. Only in Zimbabwe do the numbers of male and female migrants approach anything like equality, although males are still in the majority. Zimbabwe represents something of a special case. The country's economic, social and political breakdown makes migration a key liveli-hood strategy. Diminishing alternatives are pushing people from across the full range of age, skills and education levels, and both men and women, to engage in various forms of cross-border economic activity, from informal trade to long-term formal employment.

Table 1: Sex of Migrants		
Country	Male	Female
Lesotho	83.6	16.4
Mozambique	93.6	6.2
Swaziland	92.4	7.6
Zimbabwe	56.4	43.6
Total	84.5	15.5
N	3972	731

Swaziland and Mozambique experience low levels of female migration, with over 90% of the migrants from each country being men. While still low relative to men, at only 16.4%, Lesotho has relatively more female migrants than either Swaziland or Mozambique. In the Lesotho case, female migration is a response to male labour retrenchment from the South African mines; the relative proximity of South African towns to the Lesotho border allowing opportunities for women to engage in trading activity and domestic service; a lack of alternative livelihood strategies and economic opportunities rural and urban areas; and the relative ease of crossing the Lesotho-South Africa border.[18]

Without reliable, regular data on levels of female migration at earlier dates, it is difficult to reliably assess the extent to which female migration from any of the four countries has increased in either absolute or relative terms. What evidence there is suggests that women's migration is on the rise, within the context of a significant overall increase in regional cross-border migration since the end of apartheid.[19] Yet cross-border migration, especially formal labour migration, remains strongly male-dominated, with women still in the minority.

The MARS findings do suggest that there are significant inter-country and inter-gender differences, as well as changes over time, in migrants' demographic attributes of relationship to their household head, age and marital status (Tables 2, 3 and 4). The data points to an overall rise in the proportion of cross-border migrants who are heads of households. Interestingly, the pattern for female migrants appears to be the opposite. In all four countries, and especially in Mozambique and Swaziland, the category containing the highest proportion of female migrants is 'daughter' – almost three-quarters of the female migrants in Mozambique and two-thirds in Swaziland. Among female migrants, Swaziland and Mozambique thus most closely conform to the historical pattern of migration to South Africa dominated by young, unmarried adults. This is also true of male migrants from Mozambique.

On the male side of the equation it is striking that a large proportion of male migrants are household heads – by far the majority of male migrants in both Lesotho and Swaziland (Table 2). In Zimbabwe, the proportion of migrants who are household heads and adult sons is virtually the same. Gender analysis of earlier SAMP surveys showed that women migrants were more likely to be spouses than the adult children of the household head, while male migrants were more likely to be adult children rather than heads of household.[20] MARS suggests that this has changed, and that migration has increased among older, married, male heads of household and among younger, unmarried women.

In Lesotho, a significant proportion of women migrants (24%) are heads of their household. Zimbabwe and Lesotho also have higher proportions of women among their migrants than Swaziland or Mozambique, suggesting that female migration and female household headship are closely linked. The absence of a male household head appears to encourage female migration, perhaps because of a lack of local livelihood or employment options for women or due to the absence of patriarchal restriction on women's migration by a male spouse. Compared to Swaziland and Mozambique, Lesotho and Zimbabwe also have relatively higher proportions of female migrants in the category of 'spouse' of the household head, possibly an indication of greater social acceptance of married women's migration, even if only out of economic necessity.

Table 2: Relationship of Migrants to Head of Household								
Relation	Lesotho		Mozambique		Swaziland		Zimbabwe	
	Males (%)	Females (%)	Males (%)	Females (%)	Males (%)	Females (%)	Males (%)	Females (%)
Head	76.5	24.0	37.6	4.5	61.2	4.2	35.7	16.6
Spouse/ partner	0.1	18.4	3.5	6.1	0.2	7.3	2.1	26.7
Son/daughter	21.8	45.4	49.3	74.3	32.8	65.6	36.7	34.0
Father/mother	0.0	1.0	0.6	1.5	0.2	2.1	0.2	1.4
Brother/sister	0.5	1.5	6.8	9.1	3.3	10.4	15.1	13.6
Grandchild	0.4	1.5	0.6	0.0	1.3	7.3	0.6	0.0
Grandparent	0.0	0.0	0.0	0.0	0.0	0.0	0.0	0.0
Son/daughter-in-law	0.1	5.1	0.1	3.0	0.1	3.1	1.4	1.4
Nephew/niece	0.0	0.5	0.8	1.5	0.6	0.0	2.3	2.8
Other relative	0.6	2.6	0.6	0.0	0.3	0.0	4.6	3.5
Non-relative	0.0	0.0	0.1	0.0	0.0	0.0	1.4	0.0
Total	100	100	100	100	100	100	100	100
N	934	196	943	66	1076	96	518	427

Data on migrants' age show similar patterns and trends. The 'middle' age cohort of 25 to 39 contains the most migrants (male and female) overall (Table 3). However, the proportion of female migrants falling in the younger, 15-24 bracket is significantly higher than the equivalent proportion for males in Lesotho, Mozambique and Swaziland (i.e. all countries except Zimbabwe). In these three countries, men are correspondingly over-represented in the older, 40-59 age bracket compared to women. The differences are especially striking in Mozambique and Swaziland, with Mozambique having a particularly young female migrant cohort.

These findings are a little surprising in the light of earlier SAMP evidence that women migrants were on average older than male migrants, and may signal a significant social and demographic shift in regional migration behaviour.[21] They certainly suggest a growing feminization of migration among young adults, whereas among men there is a growing practice of migration as a long-term 'career path' rather than a temporary phase at a particular life stage.

Table 3: Age of Migrants								
Age group	Lesotho		Mozambique		Swaziland		Zimbabwe	
	Males (%)	Females (%)	Males (%)	Females (%)	Males (%)	Females (%)	Males (%)	Females (%)
15 to 24	5.4	9.7	10.3	22.7	3.0	12.5	15.3	16.2
25 to 39	41.6	41.3	48.4	36.4	44.7	57.3	57.9	54.0
40 to 59	47.3	37.2	18.1	1.5	42.9	26.0	21.2	25.8
60 and over	3.1	4.1	1.1	0.0	1.8	0.0	0.8	1.2
Don't know	2.6	7.7	22.1	39.4	7.6	4.2	4.8	2.8
Total	100	100	100	100	100	100	100	100
N	934	196	943	66	1076	96	518	427

The striking gender difference in the marital status of migrants provides further insight into the possible motives for migration (Table 4). A much higher proportion of female migrants are unmarried compared to male migrants. This is especially true of Mozambique and Swaziland, where over 50% of female migrants are unmarried. In Lesotho and Zimbabwe the figure is roughly a quarter. This suggests that some young women, whether by choice or necessity, are selecting migration over marriage as their means of support, or at least delaying marriage until later.[22]

Table 4: Marital Status of Migrants								
Marital status	Lesotho		Mozambique		Swaziland		Zimbabwe	
	Males (%)	Females (%)	Males (%)	Females (%)	Males (%)	Females (%)	Males (%)	Females (%)
Unmarried	9.7	25.0	23.9	52.3	17.5	56.3	33.5	28.3
Married	84.2	26.5	56.7	27.7	79.6	42.7	62.0	53.4
Cohabiting	0.3	0.5	16.1	9.2	1.3	0	1.0	0.5
Divorced	0	4.6	1.3	3.1	0.3	0	1.5	6.1
Separated	1.7	15.3	0.5	0	0.2	0	0.4	2.8
Abandoned	0.2	3.6	0.4	4.6	0.1	0	0.2	0.9
Widowed	3.9	24.5	1.1	3.1	1.0	1.0	1.0	8.0
Total	100	100	100	100	100	100	100	100
N	934	196	943	66	1076	96	518	427

In Lesotho, Mozambique and Zimbabwe, female migrants have higher levels of divorce, separation, abandonment and widowhood than their male counterparts. This suggests that marital breakdown or loss of a husband act as significant drivers of female migration – or, conversely, that women's migration contributes to marital breakdown. These women are likely to be the primary or sole breadwinner for their families. Again, only in Zimbabwe do the male and female profiles approach equivalence, although still with a higher percentage of migrant men being married.

Zimbabwean women migrants are more likely to be married than those from any of the other countries, while Lesotho displays an extremely high incidence of widowhood among women migrants, at 24.5%. Overall, male migrants are most likely to be married, while female migrants are for the most part without husbands, either because they have not yet or never married, or because their husbands have left them or died. This has implications for who becomes the main recipient of migrant remittances: likely the spouses of married men or women; parents (and children) of unmarried sons or daughters; and children, siblings or parents of widows or divorcees.

The education profile of migrants reveals further differences between male and female migrants, as well as amongst the four countries (Table 5). Whereas the age and marital profile of female migrants appears to have recently shifted towards more younger, unmarried women, the relatively higher educational status of female migrants appears to have persisted. Certainly in Lesotho and Swaziland, men are over-represented in the categories of 'none' or 'primary' education, while women migrants are more likely than men to have some secondary schooling. With close to three quarters of both male and female migrants having only primary education, Mozambique has the least educated migrants of the four countries. In Swaziland, over 75% of female migrants have at least

17

some secondary education, whereas in Lesotho it is just over one third. Swaziland's migrants are relatively better-educated than their Lesotho or Mozambique counterparts.

Table 5: Educational Status of Migrants								
Educational level	Lesotho		Mozambique		Swaziland		Zimbabwe	
	Males (%)	Females (%)	Males (%)	Females (%)	Males (%)	Females (%)	Males (%)	Females (%)
None	16.0	2.0	7.5	12.1	13.7	5.2	0.6	0.7
Primary	61.5	56.7	71.7	71.2	38.6	17.7	1.9	6.8
Secondary	20.3	34.7	15.4	10.6	41.8	51.1	41.0	52.7
Diploma	0.7	0.5	0.0	0.0	2.8	12.5	29.0	24.5
Degree	0.1	1.0	0.0	0.0	1.1	12.5	22.7	11.8
Postgraduate degree	0.1	1.5	0.0	0.0	0.1	1.0	4.4	2.8
Don't know	1.3	3.6	5.4	6.1	1.9	0.0	0.4	0.7
Total	100	100	100	100	100	100	100	100
N	934	196	943	66	1076	96	518	427

The Zimbabwe case again stands out as somewhat exceptional, with a far higher level of education across the migrant cohort, including significant numbers of men and women with diplomas or degrees. Less than 1% of Zimbabwean migrants of either gender have no education, and less than 10% have only primary education – further evidence of the significant skills loss being experienced by that country.[23] Even in the other three countries, the number of migrant women with secondary education, diplomas and degrees contradicts the popular stereotype of the poor, unskilled African migrant scrambling desperately across the border into South Africa.[24] In reality, it is still the more educated women who are engaging in cross-border economic migration.

In sum, the basic gender breakdown of the socio-demographic profile of migrants in the MARS data provides evidence that cross-border migration is increasingly practiced by older, married, male household heads and by younger, unmarried women. Migration is also significant among divorced, abandoned or widowed women, who find themselves in the position of head of household and in need of a means of livelihood for themselves and their families.

ATTRIBUTES OF MIGRANT-SENDING HOUSEHOLDS

Migrants are members of households in which they occupy different positions and fulfill different roles. Households themselves have particular gender, age and generational configurations. They can be male- or female-headed, nuclear or extended; and can send male and/or female migrants. By comparing household attributes, and considering individual migrants in their household context, further insights into migration and remittance behaviour in the region are made possible. Not only do male and female migrants differ in their socio-demographic profile, but they come from very different sorts of household.

Some households send multiple migrants, including both men and women, but the majority surveyed by MARS sent either only male or only female migrants (Table 6). The overall predominance of male migrants is clear, but so too are differences amongst the four countries. Zimbabwe, for example, not only has a higher proportion of female migrants relative to the other countries but a far higher proportion of migrant-sending households having both male and female members who migrate (17%). This underlines the importance of cross-border migration to the livelihoods of families in Zimbabwe, with many households sending multiple members of both genders.

Table 6: Migrant-Sending Households by Gender of Migrants			
	Male migrant-sending (%)	Female migrant-sending (%)	Male and female migrant-sending (%)
Lesotho	82.4	13.7	3.9
Mozambique	91.4	2.5	6.1
Swaziland	91.9	4.2	3.9
Zimbabwe	47.1	35.9	17.0

Swaziland and Lesotho have the lowest proportion of households sending both male and female migrants (less than 5%). Lesotho, though, has a higher proportion of households sending only women migrants (14%). Swaziland's migrant-sending households are overwhelmingly dominated by male out-migration. Its female migrants are almost as likely to come from households sending both male and female migrants as female migrants alone. Mozambique's migrant-sending households are also dominated by male-only migration, but there migrant women are slightly more likely to hail from households sending both male and female migrants than from those with only female migrant members.[25]

Unsurprisingly, the two countries reporting the highest incidence of female migration, namely Zimbabwe and Lesotho, also reported the highest incidence of female household headship, at 22.2% and 16.1% respectively (Table 7). The figures for Mozambique and Swaziland are only fractionally lower, however.

Table 7: Gender of Migrant-Sending Household Heads

	N	Male (%)	Female (%)
Lesotho	1026	83.9	16.1
Mozambique	726	84.2	15.8
Swaziland	1003	85.4	14.6
Zimbabwe	733	77.8	22.2

More revealing is a breakdown of household type by whether the migrants themselves are male or female (Table 8). Migrant-sending households can be divided into:

- Female-centred households: No husband/male partner; may include relatives, children, friends
- Male-centred households: No wife/female partner; may include relatives, children, friends
- Nuclear households: Man and woman with or without children
- Extended households: Man and woman and children and other relatives

Table 8: Household Type of Migrant-Sending Households

Household type	Lesotho		Mozambique		Swaziland		Zimbabwe	
	Male migrant-sending (%)	Female migrant-sending (%)	Male migrant-sending (%)	Female migrant-sending (%)	Male migrant-sending (%)	Female migrant-sending (%)	Male migrant-sending (%)	Female migrant-sending (%)
Female centred	7.0	42.8	10.7	41.2	17.2	31.0	11.7	28.1
Male centred	3.8	0.7	4.0	17.6	13.9	16.7	11.7	5.5
Nuclear	43.3	18.6	24.1	11.8	39.9	26.2	49.2	37.9
Extended	45.9	37.9	61.2	29.4	28.6	26.1	25.9	23.8
Other	0.0	0.0	0.0	0.0	0.4	0.0	1.5	4.7
Total	100	100	100	100	100	100	100	100
N	841	140	626	17	919	42	332	253

In Lesotho, Mozambique and Swaziland, female migrants come predominantly from female-centred households, in which there is no husband or male partner either present or living away. The proportion is highest for Lesotho, where 42.8% of households sending female migrants are female-centred. Even in Zimbabwe the proportion is high at 28.1%, not dissimilar from Swaziland's 31%. In both Lesotho and Mozambique, nuclear-family households are less likely than extended-family households to send female migrants. In Swaziland, nuclear- and extended-family households are equally likely to send female members as migrants, if still less than the proportion for female-centred households. Only in Zimbabwe are nuclear-family households the main source of female migrants, further evidence of migration becoming increasingly standard practice amongst 'ordinary' Zimbabwean families.

Households sending male migrants tend to be extended-family households in Mozambique but nuclear-family households in Swaziland and Zimbabwe, with roughly equal proportions of nuclear- and extended-family households sending male migrants from Lesotho. In all countries except Zimbabwe, where nuclear families predominate, individual households sending both male and female migrants tend to be either large, extended family households who can afford to send more members as migrants, or female-centred households also sending younger male members as migrants.

Female migration thus appears to be related to particular household forms, with female-headed or female-centred households being the source of many female migrants. These findings reinforce those described above in relation to the age, household position and marital status of male and female migrants. Male migrants are largely the middle-aged heads of 'traditional' extended- or nuclear-family households; female migrants are mostly unmarried women, along with widows and divorcees, from various forms of female-centred or female-only household. The correlation between women's migration and female household headship, or at least of various non-traditional female-centred household forms, is clear.

If female migration is indeed increasing, then it is likely that this reflects an increase in the number of female-centred households. Causes of female headship might include women delaying or avoiding marriage; incidences of divorce and abandonment; or deaths of male partners. Marital breakdown may be on the rise, as is widowhood in the context of the region's HIV-AIDS epidemic. Shifts in the labour market leading to new opportunities for women and a decline in employment for men in certain production sectors, such as mining, may be changing the economic basis of the marital bargain, making the presence of a male household head less of an economic necessity. Whether by free will or force of circumstance, many Southern African women appear to be choosing migration and avoiding marriage (or remarriage), at least in its traditional patriarchal form, while male migration appears to be being incorporated into the reproduction of traditional family and household forms. This makes female migrants' remittances far from a source of 'pin money' supplementing income earned by a male partner. Rather, women's remittances are an essential component of the livelihoods both of individual women and of the household members who depend on them.

PATTERNS OF MALE AND FEMALE MIGRATION

The geography of male and female migration in Southern Africa is heavily dominated by flows to South Africa, the region's most populous nation as well as its dominant economic power. South Africa not only has the best employment prospects, but has the largest variety of goods for purchase, consumption or trade as well. It is also the largest and most affluent market for migrants with commodities to sell. For Zimbabweans, South Africa (along with countries overseas) is a source of foreign currency to hedge against hyper-inflation and the country's collapsing dollar.

Over 90% of migrants from Lesotho, Mozambique and Swaziland live and work in South Africa (Tables 9 and 10). There is a small gender difference, with the proportion of migrant men in South Africa being slightly higher than migrant women. A correspondingly higher proportion of migrant women are in other countries. Lesotho's migration is almost entirely to South Africa, as is that of Swazi men, partly a reflection of the significance of mine labour migration. Mozambique sends small numbers of migrants, especially women, to Swaziland, Botswana and other countries in addition to South Africa. Some women migrants from Swaziland can be found in countries beyond the region. These are most likely more skilled migrants. A quarter of Swazi women migrants have diplomas or degrees. They include health workers and other professionals with internationally marketable skills.

Table 9: Current Place of Residence of Migrant Members of Household								
Place of residence	Lesotho		Mozambique		Swaziland		Zimbabwe	
	Males (%)	Females (%)	Males (%)	Females (%)	Males (%)	Females (%)	Males (%)	Females (%)
This household	0.4	0.0	1.4	0.0	2.7	3.1	26.4	30.2
This village	0.0	0.0	0.1	0.0	0.1	0.0	0.0	0.2
Nearby village	0.0	0.0	0.0	0.0	0.1	0.0	0.8	0.0
Capital city	0.0	0.0	0.0	0.0	0.0	1.0	1.7	0.5
Other urban area	0.0	0.0	0.0	0.0	0.4	1.0	3.1	1.6
Other rural area	0.0	0.0	0.0	0.0	0.0	0.0	0.6	0.2
South Africa	99.6	99.0	96.3	90.9	96.0	87.6	19.3	16.4
Other country	0.0	1.0	2.2	9.1	0.7	7.3	48.1	50.7
Don't know	0.0	0.0	0.0	0.0	0.0	0.0	0.0	0.2
Total	100	100	100	100	100	100	100	100
N	934	196	943	66	1076	96	523	427

The pattern for Zimbabwe is quite different from that of the other three countries. Migrants from Zimbabwe are more widespread across the region, especially in Botswana, as well as further afield (Table 10). Only one third of Zimbabwean migrants are in South Africa, with close to 40% of both male and female migrants working in countries outside the region. Again, this reflects the higher education and skills levels of Zimbabwean migrants, and is further evidence of the forces driving increasing numbers into the country's growing global diaspora.

While gender differences for Zimbabwe are small, there is a slightly higher proportion of migrant male Zimbabweans in South Africa and migrant Zimbabwean women in other countries. Another intriguing finding is the frequency with which the place of residence for migrant household members in the Zimbabwe survey was given as 'in this household.' This suggests that many Zimbabwean migrants engage in to-and-fro, circular migration, combining multiple livelihood strategies in different locations and engaging in various forms of mobile moonlighting. In a context where professional salaries are inadequate to meet even basic household expenses, it is not uncommon for people such as schoolteachers to maintain their jobs at home while also engaging in informal trade or temporary employment outside Zimbabwe in order to supplement their incomes and support their families.

Table 10: Country of Work of Migrants								
Country of work	Lesotho		Mozambique		Swaziland		Zimbabwe	
	Males (%)	Females (%)	Males (%)	Females (%)	Males (%)	Females (%)	Males (%)	Females (%)
Botswana	0.1	0.5	0.7	1.5	0.2	0.0	15.5	17.8
Lesotho	0.0	0.0	0.0	0.0	0.0	0.0	0.0	0.2
Malawi	0.0	0.0	0.1	0.0	0.0	0.0	0.6	1.2
Mozambique	0.0	0.0	0.0	0.0	0.1	0.0	5.2	5.2
Namibia	0.0	0.0	0.0	0.0	0.0	0.0	1.5	0.7
South Africa	99.9	99.5	96.8	91.0	98.9	86.5	34.2	30.0
Swaziland	0.0	0.0	2.1	4.5	0.0	0.0	0.2	0.0
Tanzania	0.0	0.0	0.0	0.0	0.0	0.0	0.2	0.2
Zambia	0.0	0.0	0.0	0.0	0.0	0.0	3.1	1.6
Zimbabwe	0.0	0.0	0.0	0.0	0.1	0.0	0.0	0.0
Other country	0.0	0.0	0.3	3.0	0.7	13.5	39.5	43.1
Total	100	100	100	100	100	100	100	100
N	934	196	944	66	1076	96	523	427

There are significant gender differences in the length of time individuals have been migrants (Table 11). Although some women have been migrating for over a decade, most female migration from Lesotho, Mozambique and Swaziland is relatively recent. The vast majority have less than ten years migratory experience and around half have less than five years experience. Female migration thus appears to be recent and increasing. In the case of Zimbabwe, both male and female migration are comparatively recent. Over 90% of migrants have less than 10 years migratory experience, further evidence that migration is a response to the country's slide into economic and political decline over the last decade.

Table 11: Length of Migratory Experience								
Number of years	Lesotho		Mozambique		Swaziland		Zimbabwe	
	Males (%)	Females (%)	Males (%)	Females (%)	Males (%)	Females (%)	Males (%)	Females (%)
1-5	29.2	59.5	30.4	50.0	23.6	47.6	71.1	72.5
6-10	16.3	23.4	31.2	24.0	24.4	32.1	20.9	20.5
11-15	15.0	6.3	18.7	14.0	19.8	13.1	4.6	4.3
16-20	13.6	3.4	18.4	8.0	17.6	3.6	1.4	1.9
21-25	10.5	3.4	0.0	0.0	9.0	1.2	1.2	0.3
26-30	9.5	2.3	0.0	0.0	4.7	2.4	0.2	0.0
>30	5.8	1.1	0.0	0.0	0.7	0.0	0.4	0.0
Don't know	0.1	0.6	1.3	4.0	0.2	0.0	0.2	0.5
Total	100	100	100	100	100	100	100	100
N	892	175	792	50	1018	84	483	370

OCCUPATIONS OF MALE AND FEMALE MIGRANTS

Perhaps the greatest difference between male and female migrants is in their activity and employment profiles (Table 12). Minework is still the predominant form of employment for male migrants from Lesotho, Swaziland and Mozambique, as it has been for the last century.[26] Almost 80% of male migrants from Lesotho and two-thirds from Swaziland work on the South African mines. In the case of Mozambique, the figure is one-third. Migrants from Mozambique do work in a broader range of occupations including skilled and unskilled manual labour (18%). In general, women migrants are spread across a wider range of occupations than their male counterparts. No single occupation for migrant women approaches the dominance of mining for migrant men. In the case of Lesotho, though, there is a degree of concentration with 50% of female migrants employed in domestic service.

Occupation	Lesotho		Mozambique		Swaziland		Zimbabwe	
	Males (%)	Females (%)	Males (%)	Females (%)	Males (%)	Females (%)	Males (%)	Females (%)
Farmer	0.1	1.0	0.1	1.6	0.4	1.0	1.4	0.0
Agricultural worker	1.4	4.6	2.1	3.1	0.6	1.0	0.6	1.8
Service worker	0.7	3.1	1.1	3.1	2.2	8.3	8.9	9.9
Domestic worker	0.4	50.1	0.6	4.7	0.4	14.7	0.6	4.0
Managerial office worker	0.1	0.5	0.0	0.0	0.7	4.2	4.7	1.9
Office worker	0.2	0.5	0.3	1.6	1.2	8.3	5.2	4.5
Foreman	0.1	0.0	0.5	0.0	0.7	0.0	1.0	0.2
Mineworker	80.0	2.0	32.5	0.0	66.3	0.0	5.0	0.2
Skilled manual	7.4	4.6	8.3	3.1	6.2	6.3	5.8	3.1
Unskilled manual	1.6	2.0	10.1	3.1	8.0	6.3	2.1	1.9
Informal sector producer	2.1	8.7	0.4	6.3	0.5	2.1	3.3	6.4
Trader/hawker/vendor	1.0	7.1	4.9	17.2	0.2	8.3	10.3	22.0
Security personnel	0.2	0.0	0.5	0.0	2.1	1.0	0.2	0.0
Police/military	0.0	0.5	0.1	0.0	0.0	2.1	0.8	0.0
Business (self-employed)	0.4	5.6	3.4	12.5	1.0	2.1	5.4	2.6
Employer/manager	0.0	0.0	0.0	0.0	0.1	3.1	1.7	0.5
Professional	2.8	4.6	1.8	0.0	2.6	13.5	18.5	10.1
Teacher	0.1	0.5	0.0	1.6	0.7	2.1	6.4	7.1
Health worker	0.0	1.5	0.3	0.0	0.4	2.1	6.4	16.5
Pensioner	0.1	0.0	0.0	0.0	0.0	0.0	0.0	0.0
Shepherd	0.6	0.0	0.0	0.0	0.0	0.0	0.0	0.0
Housework (unpaid)	0.0	0.0	0.0	1.6	0.0	0.0	0.0	0.0
Scholar/student	0.0	0.0	0.0	0.0	0.0	1.0	1.6	0.9
Other	0.0	0.0	17.5	7.8	3.9	9.4	3.5	1.9
Don't know	0.7	3.1	15.5	32.7	1.8	3.1	6.6	4.5
Total	100	100	100	100	100	100	100	100
N	934	196	932	64	1075	96	516	425

Table 12: Current Occupation of Migrants

Differences between countries are as striking as differences between genders. Once again, Zimbabwe is the most distinctive. Significant numbers of Zimbabwean migrants, both male and female, are employed in professional occupations, including education and health. This can be attributed to the much higher educational status and internationally marketable skills of male and female Zimbabwean migrants. Trade is also an important occupation for both. The top three occupational categories for male Zimbabwean migrants are professional, trader and service worker, and for Zimbabwean women, trader, health worker and professional.[27]

The top occupations of women from the other three countries are domestic service, informal sector production and trading for Lesotho; trading, self-employment and informal sector production for Mozambique; and domestic service, professional and service work/office work/trading in Swaziland. The occupational profile of Swaziland's migrant women displays considerable spread across categories, with a higher proportion of migrants in the categories of professional or office work relative to Lesotho, Mozambique or even Zimbabwe. The occupations of a high proportion of migrants from Mozambique are unknown to the household member completing the survey. This may reflect a higher degree of informality and flexibility among Mozambican migrants, or alternatively a lack of contact between migrants and their families.

Geographical and gender differences mean that it is impossible to generalize the survey findings across the region, although they do allow for some overall observations. Trading is clearly a significant economic activity for female migrants from all four countries, with trade being particularly important as an occupation for women from Mozambique and Zimbabwe. Domestic service is a more significant form of employment for women from Lesotho and Swaziland. Informal sector production is another important occupation for female migrants. Agricultural, manual and 'other service' work occupy a small but significant number of migrant women.

Among more skilled women, professional and office occupations are common. Overall, relative to male migrants, female migrants are less likely to be in formal employment and more likely to be engaged in informal economic activity, especially trade. Even when women are in formal employment, this is more likely to be in sectors such as domestic service than corporate labour, and thus less likely to be long-term, secure or unionized. Given this gender difference in occupation and employment, any similarities or differences between men and women in their remittance practices, and in the extent to which their households depend on those remittances, are of interest.

GENDER DIFFERENCES IN REMITTANCE FLOWS

W hat is the volume and nature of migrant remittances and their impact on household members in migrant source countries? Do these characteristics and impacts vary with gender? In order to compare male and female remittance behaviour, and the impact of remittances on sending households, it is necessary to isolate households that send migrants of either one gender or the other, but not both.

Household-level data is presented here on (a) whether migrants send money home, and how much; (b) whether migrant remittances are a primary source of household income; (c) the main household expenditures; (d) what remittance money is spent on; (e) whether migrants send more in times of crisis or need; and (f) the perceived importance of remittances to the household. What is perhaps most striking is the enormous significance of migrant remittances to household subsistence and material needs. This is true irrespective of whether the migrants are male or female, although there are some inter-gender as well as inter-country differences.

The importance of remittances is evident in the straightforward proportion of migrant-sending households that receive money from their migrant members (Table 13). At close to 90% for Lesotho, Swaziland and Zimbabwe, this is an extremely high figure in international comparative terms. Mozambique is a slight exception, with a lower proportion of households receiving remittances. Nevertheless, the majority (80% of male migrant-sending households and 60% of female migrant-sending households) do still receive remittances. The demographic profile of migrants from Mozambique might suggest that daughters are less likely to send money home than sons, and adult children overall less likely to send money home than heads of household or their spouses. However, the Mozambican female sample is too small to be definitive.

Table 13: Proportion of Households Receiving Remittances		
Country	Male migrant-sending households (%)	Female migrant-sending households (%)
Lesotho	94.9	89.3
Mozambique	79.6	58.8
Swaziland	88.8	92.9
Zimbabwe	89.5	90.1

In Swaziland and Lesotho, there are small differences between the sexes. Male migrants from Lesotho are slightly more likely to remit than female migrants and female migrants are slightly more likely to remit than male migrants from Swaziland. At least in part, this reflects the differential earning power of male and female migrants from the two countries. Once again, the figures for Zimbabwe are essentially the same for male and female migrants.

The amounts of money remitted by female migrants are significantly lower than those of male migrants, however (Table 14). Women's employment and livelihood strategies – for example as informal sector traders or domestic workers compared to waged mine labour – mean lower earnings overall and less regular or reliable remuneration than their male counterparts. In addition, female migrants who are daughters rather than spouses or heads of household may choose to remit a lower proportion of their earnings compared to male migrants, who are more likely to be heads of household and primary income-earners.

Table 14: Average Annual Remittances Received from Male and Female Migrants		Male migrants	Female migrants
Lesotho	Mean	R11,162.46	R4,825.32
	Median	R9,600.00	R3,600.00
Mozambique	Mean	R2,929.78	R452.53
	Median	R2,011.25	R301.69
Swaziland	Mean	R4,714.12	R5,351.85
	Median	R2,400.00	R1,800.00
Zimbabwe	Mean	R2,947.81	R2,044.71
	Median	R1,092.99	R1,092.99

Gender differences in remittances are most stark in Lesotho and Mozambique. Swaziland's gender-differentiated remittance data shows higher mean but lower median remittances by female migrants (Table 14).[28] This reflects the education and employment profile of Swaziland's female migrants, which includes a small but significant number of well-educated women working in professional occupations. Their earnings skew the mean value upward. Comparing median values thus gives a more representative overall picture of relative male and female remittances. Zimbabwe's more gender-equivalent migration profile is again borne out in the remittance data. Zimbabwean migrant men and women occupy more similar occupational categories than men and women from the other countries, and are thus more likely to have equivalent earnings and remit similar amounts.

Exchange rate variations and differences in purchasing power parity make inter-country comparisons of remittance values difficult - except in the case of Lesotho and Swaziland, each of which has a fixed 1:1 exchange rate with the South African Rand. That said, migrants from Lesotho do seem to remit considerably more than migrants from the other countries. This is partly explained by the fact that the South African mining industry employs so many Basotho migrants. However, female migrants from Lesotho also remit more than female migrants from the other three countries. This could reflect differences in earning power. Equally, it could be because the need for livelihoods-based remitting is greater in Lesotho.

Gender differences diminish considerably when remittances are considered in terms of their contribution to the household economy, rather than their absolute monetary value. Migrant remittances form an important, and in many cases the only, source of income for many households (Table 15).[29] In each country, remittances are listed by significantly more households than any other single income source. Other findings include:

- Lesotho has the highest incidence of households reporting remittance earnings, followed by Zimbabwe, Mozambique and Swaziland. Wage work, casual work and informal business were the only other significant sources of household income in the Lesotho sample, all falling well below remittances. Migration is not merely a supplementary livelihood strategy but the principal source of household income.
- Zimbabwe has the highest proportion of its migrant-sending households with multiple sources of income, with more than 50% reporting domestic wage labour earnings in addition to remittances. Income from business (formal or informal) or casual work is also important.
- Mozambican households also have a high incidence of multiple income sources, especially from informal business, casual work and farm product sales, supplementing remittance earnings.
- In Swaziland, local wage labour and informal business were sources of income for a significant proportion of migrants' households.
- Zimbabwe and Mozambique recorded the highest incidence of the remittance of goods.

For many households from Zimbabwe, Mozambique and Swaziland, migration does seem to be part of a bundle of livelihood strategies, if not an important one, combined with other, local sources of income.

Table 15: Sources of Household Income in Male and Female Migrant-Sending Households

Source of household income	Lesotho		Mozambique		Swaziland		Zimbabwe	
	Male migrant-sending (%)	Female migrant-sending (%)	Male migrant-sending (%)	Female migrant-sending (%)	Male migrant-sending (%)	Female migrant-sending (%)	Male migrant-sending (%)	Female migrant-sending (%)
Wage work	8.3	15.0	32.7	47.0	46.1	42.9	58.1	56.9
Casual work	5.0	12.1	12.8	29.4	2.3	4.8	14.2	9.1
Remittances – money	95.7	90.0	77.3	64.7	63.2	64.3	84.6	77.9
Remittances – goods	19.6	22.8	64.5	64.7	16.1	16.7	62.0	71.5
Farm product sales	2.4	2.8	21.6	5.9	9.7	7.1	7.2	7.9
Formal business	2.1	1.4	3.5	11.8	2.4	4.8	9.3	8.7
Informal business	6.5	6.4	22.4	23.5	13.1	14.3	13.6	19.4
Pension/ disability	0.2	2.1	2.4	11.8	1.9	7.1	7.5	7.5
Gifts	2.4	1.4	3.0	5.9	3	0	4.2	6.3
Other	0	0	3.2	5.9	0.8	2.4	0.6	2.8
Refused to answer	0	0	1.4	5.9	0.3	0	2.4	1.6
Don't know	0.5	2.1	0.6	0	0.4	2.4	1.8	5.5
N	841	140	626	17	919	42	332	253

Note: Because many households had more than one source of income, percentages add up to more than 100%.

Such bundling seems to be especially true of households sending female migrants, more of which reported multiple sources of income compared to male-sending households. This is unsurprising given that female migrants remit lower sums, making other income sources a necessity. They are also less likely to be household heads, which means that they are often members of households with other working adult members. Male migrant remittances, by contrast, are more likely to be the primary or sole source of income for their households. In Lesotho, for example, over 95% of households with male migrant members list remittances as a source of household income. Under 10% list income from the second-ranking income source, non-migrant wage labour. The equivalent proportions for female-sending households in Lesotho are around 90% and 15%. Lesotho, it should be recalled, is the country with the highest proportion of male and female migrants giving their status as head of household, making the migrants more likely to be their family's primary, or sole, breadwinner.

In Mozambique and Zimbabwe, as in Lesotho, households with male migrants are more likely to list monetary remittances as a source of income than households sending female migrants. In Zimbabwe, 85% of male-migrant and 78% of female migrant-sending households report remittances as an income source, while for Mozambique the equivalent proportions were 77% and 65%. Swaziland shows remarkable similarities in the incidence of remittance earnings from male and female migrants, at 63% and 64% respectively. These gender differences are counterbalanced somewhat by female migrants' higher levels of remittance of goods. The proportion of female migrants sending home goods is higher than the equivalent proportion of male migrants, especially in Zimbabwe and to a lesser extent Lesotho.

In sum, female migrant remittances are a demonstrably important source of both income and material goods for female migrant-sending households. Whether they are household heads, spouses or daughters, women migrants are clearly sending significant sums of money and quantities of goods back to their families in their home countries, contributing in no small way to those households' material welfare. This is confirmed by the more detailed exploration of the use and impact of remittances in the next section.

GENDER DIFFERENCES IN REMITTANCE USAGE

Data on household expenditures and use of remittances provides additional insight into the similarities and differences between male migrant and female migrant-sending households. The data shows small but significant gender-based differences in household expenditures (Tables 16 and 17.)[30]

The main household purchases for both male and female migrant-sending households are the basic commodities of food, domestic fuel and clothing, and fundamental services such as schooling, health care and transport. Only in Swaziland do a significant proportion of households invest money in farming. Food, medical expenses, farming and transport are most important for Swazi male migrant-sending households. Food and medical expenses are also most important for Swazi female-sending households, followed by education rather than farming. In Lesotho, the most common expenses are, in rank order, food, domestic fuel (e.g. paraffin, wood, gas), clothing, and transport. These priorities are the same for both male and female migrant-sending households. In Mozambique, food, fuel, education, and transport are most important for male migrant-sending households and food, fuel, utilities and education for female migrant-sending households. In Zimbabwe, male and female migrant-sending households report the same top four expenditures: food, utilities, education and clothing, with transport, housing and medical expenses not far behind.

Table 16: Proportion of Migrant-Sending Households Incurring Particular Expense

Expense incurred in previous month	Lesotho		Mozambique		Swaziland		Zimbabwe	
	Male migrant-sending (%)	Female migrant-sending (%)	Male migrant-sending (%)	Female migrant-sending (%)	Male migrant-sending (%)	Female migrant-sending (%)	Male migrant-sending (%)	Female migrant-sending (%)
Food/ groceries	93.3	90.0	72.2	58.8	94.0	95.2	89.2	86.9
Housing	0.7	1.4	0.3	0.0	0.4	0.0	44.3	47.4
Utilities	17.7	12.1	36.9	41.2	11.0	16.6	68.1	64.8
Clothes	73.7	68.6	28.3	23.5	15.9	19.0	51.5	50.1
Alcohol	13.0	5.7	27.8	29.4	1.2	2.4	14.5	15.8
Medical costs	26.5	12.9	27.5	17.6	39.3	33.4	36.4	38.3
Transport	54.8	39.3	37.1	23.5	37.3	28.6	45.8	47.8
Tobacco	10.9	8.6	4.6	5.9	1.0	7.1	2.7	3.2
Education	5.7	3.6	41.5	29.4	29.0	28.6	55.7	57.7
Entertainment	1.7	0.7	1.6	5.9	0.0	0.0	7.8	9.5
Savings	10.1	2.1	7.8	0.0	8.3	14.3	32.8	29.6
Fuel	77.9	69.3	41.5	47.1	30.7	26.2	5.1	4.3
Farming	7.7	4.3	9.9	5.9	39.0	23.8	6.9	5.9
Building	3.9	0.7	10.1	17.6	6.7	4.8	11.1	9.5
Special events	7.7	5.7	7.8	5.9	5.3	7.1	10.2	13.4
Gifts	3.9	2.1	4.3	5.9	0.9	0.0	2.4	4.7
Other	0.8	1.4	4.3	0.0	0.9	0.0	0.6	1.2
N	841	140	626	17	919	42	332	253

Table 17: Migrant-Sending Household Expenditures

Median Amount Spent in Previous Month (Converted to SA Rand)

	Lesotho		Mozambique		Swaziland		Zimbabwe	
	Male	Female	Male	Female	Male	Female	Male	Female
Food/groceries	400	215	251	101	300	300	55	64
Utilities	60	75	35	8	120	550	9	9
Clothes	500	350	126	148	267	375	45	45
Medical expenses	50	33	5	2	22	100	16	15
Transport	70	40	38	29	30	100	18	23
Education	230	230	30	23	400	450	45	39
Domestic fuel	90	50	20	13	48	50	3	5
Farming	350	100	75	50	600	600	91	36

In each country, the rank order of items purchased is broadly similar or even identical for male and female migrant-sending households. However, some gender differences emerge in the recorded incidence of expenditure in various categories. Gender differences are most consistent in Lesotho, where expenditure is more common in almost every category for male compared to female migrant-sending households. This could mean that in Lesotho at least, households with female migrant members (many of which were also female-centred or female-headed) are indeed poorer, and forced to 'go without' more often than households where the migrant members are men.

Gender-based patterns are more mixed in Mozambique, although lower proportions of female migrant-sending households report expenditure in the key categories of food, clothing, medical expenses, education and transport. In Swaziland, there is no clear or consistent overall difference based on migrant gender. Some differences exist in individual categories such as farming, where male migrant-sending households are more likely to report expenditure than female migrant-sending households. Savings are more common in female migrant-sending households. Zimbabwe displays the strongest similarity between expenditure in male and in female migrant-sending households, which is consistent with findings from the rest of the survey in that country.

There are important gender differences, as well as differences between countries, in the estimated monthly expenditure on particular categories of expenses (Table 17).[31] Women migrants from Lesotho and Mozambique come from households with lower monthly expenditures than households with male migrants. In these two countries the level of expenditure in most categories is lower for female migrant-sending households (except education and utilities in Lesotho and clothing in Mozambique).

Swaziland displays the opposite gender pattern to Lesotho and Mozambique. Swazi households where the migrant members are female spend more in each category than households with male migrant members. This could mean that remittances from Swazi female migrants supplement other sources of household income (including from farming). Alternatively, the higher-status and higher-paying occupational profile of Swazi women migrants could explain the difference. Swaziland (along with Mozambique) has a relatively low overall level of female migration, but those Swazi women who do migrate for work appear to come from less poor households. The significantly higher expenditure on medical costs by Swaziland's female migrant-sending households is possibly linked to the country's high rate of HIV infection.

Zimbabwe again stands out as the country with strongest gender similarity, suggesting that male and female migrants come from similar sorts of households in socio-economic terms. Further research and analysis is required to try and explain these observed gender differences in each country, but the evident contrast between countries shows the importance of gender analysis in seeking to understand the nature and role of female migration in different contexts.

Given the weighting of overall household expenditures towards basic necessities, what is the role of remittances in enabling migrant-sending households to purchase particular goods and services? Are remittances spent on the same general basket of items? Are they used for non-essential or luxury items? Or are they directed towards savings or investment in business or other productive activities?

Food is the most common annual expenditure of remittance money in all four countries and in both male- and female-migrant households (Table 18). Second in all countries is either clothing or school fees. Clothing or school fees also ranks third in all countries except Swaziland, where purchases of agricultural inputs, and in particular seed, rank above clothing. Transport fares rank fourth in Lesotho and Zimbabwe, with savings fifth in Zimbabwe and funeral policies the fifth-greatest expenditure of remittances in Lesotho. For Mozambican male-migrant households, seed ranks fourth and transport fifth, while for Mozambican households with female migrants, cement and funerals rank fourth and fifth respectively. The significance of funeral costs and policies is stark testimony to the devastating impact of HIV-AIDS.

Table 18: Ranking of Most Common Uses of Cash Remittances Over Previous Year

Lesotho		Mozambique		Swaziland		Zimbabwe	
Male migrant-sending house-holds	Female migrant-sending house-holds	Male migrant-sending house-holds	Female migrant-sending house-holds	Male migrant-sending house-holds	Female migrant-sending house-holds	Male migrant-sending house-holds	Female migrant-sending house-holds
Food	Food	Food	Food	Food	Food	Food	Food
Clothes	Clothes	Schooling	Clothes	Schooling	Schooling	Clothes	Schooling
Schooling	Schooling	Clothes	Schooling	Seed	Seed	Schooling	Clothes
Fares	Fares	Seed	Cement	Tractor	Tractor	Fares	Fares
Funeral policies	Funeral policies	Fares	Funeral	Fertiliser	Fertiliser	Savings	Savings

Remittance-receiving households confirmed the significance of remittances to food purchases (Table 19). The most consistent importance rating, across countries and migrant genders, is food, with school fees and clothes also rated highly by many. There are some gender differences, with men's remittances seemingly more crucial to the purchase of basic livelihood items such as food, than women's. Given that male migrants

are older, more likely to be married, and more often the heads of households than female migrants, it is perhaps surprising that this gender difference was not greater.

Table 19: Importance of Remittances in Annual Household Expenditure									
		Lesotho		Mozambique		Swaziland		Zimbabwe	
		Male migrant-sending (%)	Female migrant-sending (%)	Male migrant-sending (%)	Female migrant-sending (%)	Male migrant-sending (%)	Female migrant-sending (%)	Male migrant-sending (%)	Female migrant-sending (%)
Food	Very important	72.0	68.6	52.4	35.3	75.0	64.3	47.3	43.5
	Important	8.0	8.6	12.1	23.5	8.6	14.3	8.4	8.7
Clothes	Very important	53.0	50.1	14.9	5.9	17.2	16.7	23.4	22.1
	Important	21.3	12.1	18.4	23.5	4.6	4.8	12.3	13.8
Schooling	Very important	50.8	37.9	25.2	0.0	45.8	31.0	34.0	47.3
	Important	8.0	8.6	18.2	23.5	8.9	11.9	3.9	5.1
Fares	Very important	39.0	80.0	5.4	0.0	15.8	9.5	12.6	13.0
	Important	13.3	7.9	14.7	5.9	5.5	2.3	3.6	5.5
Seed	Very important	20.7	27.1	6.2	0.0	34.2	35.7	5.4	2.3
	Important	4.5	1.4	12.1	5.9	9.4	4.8	1.8	2.8
Savings	Very important	16.4	27.1	7.0	11.8	3.6	2.4	13.0	16.7
	Important	4.5	5.7	3.5	0.0	1.1	0.0	1.8	1.7
Funeral policies	Very important	19.6	59.3	0.0	0.0	0.2	0.0	3.9	2.8
	Important	9.9	5.7	0.5	0.0	0.1	0.0	2.1	0.8
Funerals	Very important	9.5	40.7	1.8	11.8	3.7	4.8	4.5	4.7
	Important	6.8	7.1	2.4	0.0	0.9	0.0	1.8	1.2
N		841	140	626	17	919	42	332	253

What stands out is the fundamental importance of remittances in
enabling migrant-sending households to meet their basic needs, such as
food and clothing, and basic services such as transport and schooling.
Remittances are used to some extent to support agricultural production
through seed purchase, but given the low reported income from farm
product sales, this must be largely for household subsistence production.
Virtually all of the households that did purchase seed said that remittances were important or very important in enabling them to make the
purchase. Remittance earnings do not appear to be 'squandered' on

luxury consumer items. In general, the pattern for expenditure of remittances reflects the patterns for overall household expenditure.

The 'typical' male or female migrant sends home money, which their households use to buy food and other basic goods and services, and brings home clothing, food and other goods (Table 20). Again, there is a striking similarity between countries and between genders. Some consumer goods and other 'luxury' items (e.g. electronic goods) are also sent home, as they are more readily available and cheaper in South Africa. Seed again shows up for Swazi migrant men. The practice of trading as a cross-border activity is revealed in the remittance of goods by Zimbabwean women for resale in their home country and the 'other goods' brought home by men and women from Mozambique.

In gender terms, the similarities in the nature and expenditure of remittances from male and female migrants are strong and revealing. Two important conclusions follow. First, for both male and female migrants, migration is commonly undertaken in the role of primary breadwinner, rather than as a supplement to other sources of household income. Second, remittances are more important as a means of securing basic household livelihoods and alleviating poverty than as drivers of broader economic development.

Table 20: Most Important Goods Remitted by Migrants							
Lesotho		Mozambique		Swaziland		Zimbabwe	
Male migrant-sending house-holds	Female migrant-sending house-holds	Male migrant-sending house-holds	Female migrant-sending house-holds	Male migrant-sending house-holds	Female migrant-sending house-holds	Male migrant-sending house-holds	Female migrant-sending house-holds
Clothes Food Consumer goods	Clothes Food Consumer goods	Food Clothes Other goods	Food Clothes Other goods	Clothes Food Seed	Clothes Food Consumer goods	Clothes Food Entertain-ment	Clothes Food Goods for resale

EMERGENCY REMITTING

In addition to making regular remittances, migrants send money home in times of need, or to meet unexpected costs. Funeral costs are by far the most common, along with funds for weddings and other feasts. Lesotho, which has the highest overall dependence on migrant remittances, has the lowest incidence of such "once-off" or emergency remittances. This may indicate that Lesotho's migrants are already sending as much as they can in routine remittances and have little to spare.

Some gender differences are evident, although this is not the same for all four countries (Table 21). In Lesotho and Mozambique, a higher proportion of male migrants send money in times of need, whereas in Swaziland female migrants are more likely to do so. This mirrors the gender differences in overall remittance behaviour. Not only are female migrants from Swaziland more likely than their male counterparts to respond to family crises with financial assistance, but the proportion of Swazi women migrants sending emergency remittances is also higher than for either men or women migrants from any of the other three countries. In Zimbabwe, once again, there is very little difference based on the gender of the migrant.

Table 21: Proportion of Households Receiving Emergency Remittances

	Male migrant-sending households (%)	Female migrant-sending households (%)
Lesotho	44.0	37.1
Mozambique	59.3	35.3
Swaziland	51.9	61.9
Zimbabwe	54.8	54.2

Emergency remittances are clearly important to the households receiving them. They are seen as important or very important by over 90% of migrant-sending households in each of the four countries, with only very small differences on the basis of migrant gender (Table 22). The importance of emergency remittances appears to be especially high to households in Swaziland and Zimbabwe, the two countries with lower reported dependence on regular remittances. This reinforces the hypothesis that migration from these two countries is practiced as part of a bundle of household livelihood strategies, making an important contribution in times of hardship, but not necessarily being the sole mainstay of household support.

Table 22: Stated Importance of Emergency Remitting to Households

		Male migrant-sending households (%)	Female migrant-sending households (%)
Lesotho	Very important	73.9	70.6
	Important	24.5	27.5
Mozambique	Very important	63.8	66.7
	Important	30.1	16.7
Swaziland	Very important	85.3	80.8
	Important	12.8	15.5
Zimbabwe	Very important	83.0	81.0
	Important	14.3	15.3

REMITTANCES AND HOUSEHOLD DEPRIVATION

Remittances are clearly essential to household subsistence and well-being. However, this does not give a sense of the nature and intensity of the poverty and deprivation still experienced by most migrants' households. To ascertain the links between remittances, migration and poverty, data was collected on 'lived poverty.' Households with migrants were asked how often they had gone without particular basic needs in the previous year (Table 23).

Table 23: Frequency of Household Deprivation of Basic Needs in Previous Year								
	Lesotho		Mozambique		Swaziland		Zimbabwe	
	Male migrant-sending (%)	Female migrant-sending (%)	Male migrant-sending (%)	Female migrant-sending (%)	Male migrant-sending (%)	Female migrant-sending (%)	Male migrant-sending (%)	Female migrant-sending (%)
Gone without: Food								
Never	48.3	32.9	32.2	52.9	38.5	61.9	68.6	69.9
Once or twice	15.3	15.7	10.0	5.9	22.5	14.3	22.0	20.1
Several times	15.2	18.6	33.3	29.4	19.3	9.5	7.6	7.2
Many times	19.6	32.1	23.3	11.8	17.1	14.3	1.5	2.4
Always	1.5	0.7	0.5	0.0	2.6	0.0	0.3	0.4
Gone without: Clean water								
Never	34.4	39.3	62.2	82.4	39.9	45.2	75.0	77.9
Once or twice	14.0	10.0	7.4	0.0	17.8	26.2	15.5	13.7
Several times	17.8	17.9	15.9	11.8	22.9	23.8	5.5	4.8
Many times	27.1	29.3	8.7	5.9	13.7	4.8	4.0	3.2
Always	6.7	3.6	5.6	0.0	5.7	0.0	0.0	0.4
Gone without: Medicine or medical treatment								
Never	37.6	32.1	45.4	47.1	38.4	54.8	71.1	74.0
Once or twice	28.2	25.7	14.6	35.3	25.1	31.0	20.9	18.3
Several times	18.3	20.7	23.3	11.8	25.2	11.9	7.1	5.3
Many times	14.3	17.9	12.0	5.9	9.6	0.0	0.6	2.0
Always	1.7	3.6	3.3	0.0	1.6	2.4	0.3	0.4
Gone without: Electricity								
Never	4.8	3.6	11.6	17.6	10.4	28.6	69.6	71.3
Once or twice	2.1	0.7	3.3	0.0	5.1	14.3	18.9	15.0
Several times	0.6	0.0	3.6	0.0	2.1	2.4	9.0	8.3
Many times	0.7	0.0	2.2	5.9	1.0	0.0	1.6	2.1
Always	91.8	95.7	79.1	76.5	73.2	42.9	1.0	3.3

Gone without: Fuel for cooking								
Never	47.9	47.1	68.8	64.7	60.8	66.7	77.7	73.2
Once or twice	21.4	20.7	7.8	17.6	18.0	19.0	14.6	17.2
Several times	14.6	12.9	18.3	17.6	13.4	9.5	5.7	5.9
Many times	15.0	17.9	3.6	0.0	4.0	2.4	1.6	2.1
Always	1.1	1.4	0.6	0.0	2.6	2.4	0.3	1.7
Gone without: Cash income								
Never	26.3	19.3	11.2	41.2	27.7	38.1	53.4	51.2
Once or twice	28.1	17.9	11.7	0.0	22.6	28.6	27.7	25.4
Several times	17.6	22.9	34.3	23.5	25.4	21.4	14.0	15.3
Many times	25.6	33.6	36.5	35.3	18.2	7.1	3.7	5.2
Always	2.4	5.7	5.7	0.0	6.1	4.8	1.2	2.8

Overall, migrant households in Lesotho and Mozambique are more deprived when compared to migrant households in Swaziland and especially Zimbabwe. Not only are migrant households more deprived in Lesotho in comparison to the other countries, but female migrant-sending households in Lesotho are relatively more deprived than male migrant-sending households. Over half (52%) of female migrant-sending households in Lesotho report going without food 'several times' or more in the previous year, compared to only 37% of male migrant-sending households. A similar pattern was found amongst Lesotho households for cash income: 63% for female migrant-sending households, 46% for male migrant-sending households.

Deprivation indices were more gender-equivalent for electricity, water and fuel, but this is more a reflection of a general lack of service provision, especially in rural areas, than of poverty per se. Even for medicine and medical treatment, female migrant-sending households are worse off than male migrant-sending households. Lesotho's female migrants (most of whom go to South Africa to work in domestic service) evidently come from very poor, severely deprived households that would likely be considerably worse off if they did not have migrant remittances as a source of income.

Mozambique's female migrant-sending households appear to be significantly less deprived in all categories, including food and income, than male migrant-sending households. This runs counter to some of the household expenditure data discussed above. In fact, Mozambican male migrant-sending households report the highest relative levels of food and income deprivation of all four countries, with 77% having gone without a cash income and 57% without food 'several times' or more in the past year. The equivalent figures for Mozambican female migrant-sending households are 59% and 41%. Certainly male migrant-sending households in Mozambique, despite receiving remittances, remain significantly deprived of even the basic means of subsistence.

Swaziland's pattern of better-off female migrant-sending households is supported by the deprivation data. There, 39% of male migrant-sending households report going without food at least 'several times' in the previous year, whereas this was true for only 24% of female migrant-sending households (less than half the equivalent for Lesotho). Income, clean water, electricity and fuel for cooking deprivation show a similar contrast. The contrast was especially strong for health care: 37% of male migrant-sending households but only 14% of female migrant-sending households report going without medicine or medical treatment in the previous year. Thus while Swaziland's male migrants seem to come from households of broadly similar socio-economic status to those in Lesotho, Swaziland's female migrants come from more affluent or less deprived households than those of male migrants from their own country

Zimbabwe's migrant households are less frequently deprived of food, income or medical treatment than migrant households in the other countries. Electricity, clean water and fuel for cooking are also available to most households most of the time. This suggests that Zimbabwe's migrants are drawn from a more urbanized and relatively better-off population than migrants from the other three countries. Gender differences, as for most of the survey findings, are also smaller in Zimbabwe. This suggests that Zimbabwe's male and female migrants are coming from the same sorts of households, rather than that female (or male) migration reflects particular gendered patterns of poverty or deprivation.

PERCEPTION OF REMITTANCE IMPACTS

In order to determine how the role and significance of migration are perceived by sending households, respondents were asked to assess the overall impact of migration on a five-point scale from very positive to very negative. They were also asked questions about the most positive and negative aspects of having household members working in another country.

Respondents in Zimbabwe are the most positive of all about migration. Close to 90% regard the impact of migration as either positive or very positive, with only a small difference based on the gender of the migrant (Table 24). Respondents in the other three countries were broadly positive, although more so for male than for female migration. Close to 70% of the male migrant-sending household respondents in Lesotho, Mozambique and Swaziland regard migration as having positive or very positive impacts. The respective values for each country's female migrant-sending households were 59%, 53% and 64%.

Table 24: Perceived Overall Impact of Migration on the Household								
	Lesotho		Mozambique		Swaziland		Zimbabwe	
	Male migrant-sending (%)	Female migrant-sending (%)	Male migrant-sending (%)	Female migrant-sending (%)	Male migrant-sending (%)	Female migrant-sending (%)	Male migrant-sending (%)	Female migrant-sending (%)
Very positive	34.4	17.9	26.7	23.5	38.9	33.3	61.5	66.7
Positive	35.2	41.5	42.7	29.4	28.8	31.0	28.5	25.5
Neither	2.3	2.1	13.2	35.3	16.6	28.6	9.7	6.6
Negative	13.9	17.1	11.6	5.9	8.8	7.1	0.3	0.0
Very negative	12.7	20.7	3.1	0.0	6.6	0.0	0.0	1.2
Don't know	1.5	0.7	2.7	5.9	0.3	0.0	0.0	0
Total	100	100	100	100	100	100	100	100
N	841	140	619	17	919	42	319	243

A surprisingly large proportion of the female migrant-sending households from Lesotho regard the impact of migration as either negative or very negative, at 38% (compared to 27% of the male migrant-sending households). Very few respondents are equivocal. This is especially interesting given the high levels of poverty and deprivation in Lesotho's female migrant-sending households and the significant contribution made by female migrant remittances to household income and expenditure. Possible explanations are that the social costs of migration outweigh its economic gains; or alternatively that female migration is indeed a 'last resort', and thus a source of shame and embarrassment to the household, especially if it is related to marital breakdown or to perceived male failure to earn a living for the family.

In Mozambique, the most common response (35%) among female migrant-sending households is that migration is neither positive nor negative. Only 6% view it as negative and none very negative. In contrast, 15% of male migrant-sending households in Mozambique are negative/very negative and only 13% are neutral. Swaziland's female migrant-sending households also have high neutral response (29%) and a low level of negative or very negative responses (7%), compared to 17% and 15% in male migrant-sending households. Thus, in both Swaziland and Mozambique, male migrant-sending households have definite opinions about the value of migration, whereas female migrant-sending households are more likely to be ambivalent. This suggests a resigned acceptance of female migration by many households.

Perceptions of the positive impacts of working in another country reinforce the findings from income, expenditure and deprivation data, i.e. migrants support their households, improve living conditions and provide household income (Table 25). In all four countries, differences based on the gender of the migrant are small (except for the fact that in three of the four, more female than male migrant-sending households report no 'most positive impact' of migration). In general, female migration is seen as providing the same sorts of benefits as male migration. This supports the finding that female migration is as economically important as male migration, at least to migrant-sending households themselves. It also emphasizes the significance of migration and related remittances to household livelihoods, and thus to poverty alleviation.

Table 25: Most Positive Effects of Migration on the Household								
	Lesotho		Mozambique		Swaziland		Zimbabwe	
	Male migrant-sending (%)	Female migrant-sending (%)	Male migrant-sending (%)	Female migrant-sending (%)	Male migrant-sending (%)	Female migrant-sending (%)	Male migrant-sending (%)	Female migrant-sending (%)
None	16.2	24.7	7.3	11.8	18.4	21.0	0.0	0.0
Supports household	6.9	5.6	35.1	41.2	29.7	46.8	30.5	31.6
Improved living conditions	63.2	58.6	6.7	0.0	<1	0.0	17.9	19.7
Able to meet basic needs	0.0	0.0	0.0	0.0	8.5	11.3	0.0	0.0
Supports children's education	11.7	11.1	0.0	0.0	15.6	6.5	0.0	0.0
Source of income	0.0	0.0	19.6	23.5	0.0	0.0	25.3	25.0
Enables purchase of goods	0.0	0.0	9.9	11.8	<1	0.0	7.4	14.5
Build/buy own house	0.0	0.0	0.0	0.0	13.2	8.1	14.7	7.9
Finances farming	0.0	0.0	0.0	0.0	13.8	6.5	0.0	0.0
Job opportunities	<1	0.0	13.4	5.9	<1	0.0	0.0	0.0
Migrant acquires skills	<1	0.0	<1	0.0	0.0	0.0	4.2	1.3
N	841	140	819	17	919	42	319	243

While the economic benefits of migration are recognized, so too are some of its social costs (Table 26). The broad patterns are the same, irrespective of whether the migrant is male or female. That so many households report no negative impacts, however, shows the generally favourable view of cross-border migration, including migration by women.

Table 26: Most Negative Effects of Migration on the Household								
	Lesotho		Mozambique		Swaziland		Zimbabwe	
	Male migrant-sending (%)	Female migrant-sending (%)	Male migrant-sending (%)	Female migrant-sending (%)	Male migrant-sending (%)	Female migrant-sending (%)	Male migrant-sending (%)	Female migrant-sending (%)
None	34.4	32.0	12.4	35.7	42.3	57.4	0.0	0.0
Loneliness	19.0	18.0	<1	0.0	0.0	0.0	50.0	37.9
Too much responsibility	13.2	8.0	9.4	7.1	0.0	0.0	9.6	10.3
Cost of living in host country	<1	<1	0.0	0.0	1.3	0.0	0.0	0.0
Earnings too little	4.8	6.0	0.0	0.0	14.3	22.2	0.0	0.0
Too far away	5.8	7.3	0.0	0.0	13.7	14.8	0.0	0.0
Lack of support for family	6.0	14.0	13.9	7.1	4.9	0.0	0.0	0.0
Away too long	0.0	1.3	30.9	28.6	0	0.0	0.0	0.0
Fear of migrant not returning	<1	0.0	<1	0.0	14.0	0.0	0.0	0.0
Lack of parental support	<1	1.3	9.8	0.0	0.4	1.9	7.7	20.7
Security in host country	0.0	0.0	4.6	7.1	2.6	0.0	0.0	0.0
Job safety risks	5.4	4.0	0.0	0.0	1.4	0.0	3.8	3.4
Infidelity or promiscuity	0.0	0.0	0.0	0.0	3.6	1.9	9.6	6.9
Migrants' poor living conditions	2.3	2.0	<1	0.0	0.0	0.0	0.0	0.0
Family's safety	3.1	2.7	0.0	0.0	<1	0.0	11.5	17.2
Homesickness of migrant	2.3	1.3	<1	0.0	<1	0.0	0.0	0.0
Bringing disease	0.0	0.0	1.1	7.1	1.1	1.9	0.0	0.0
Bad behaviour	1.2	0.0	0.0	0.0	0.0	0.0	5.8	3.4
N	921	150	540	14	1322	62	95	76

In Lesotho and Zimbabwe simple loneliness is cited as the most negative effect of migration. In Mozambique, prolonged separation is stated as migrants 'being away too long.' In Swaziland, the main concerns are that migrants earn too little, or are 'too far away.' With male migrants there is an additional fear that the migrant might never return. Not being able to provide family support and placing too much responsibility on remaining household members are also identified as negative household effects of migration. In Zimbabwe, fears were expressed by some about infidelity or other 'bad behaviour', along with concerns about family safety in the migrant's absence.

CONCLUSIONS

Remittances are clearly playing a vital role in supporting Southern African households. Not only do migrants, whether male or female, demonstrate an unusually high tendency to send money home to their families, but those remittances are fundamental in enabling families to meet their everyday needs. Remittances are the single most significant source of income for many migrant-sending households. They also act as an important safety net in times of unexpected costs or hardship.

Remittance behaviour and the role of remittances in the household economy differ only slightly based on the gender of the migrant. This demonstrates that women's migration, while lower in volume than male migration, is nevertheless highly important to the migrant-sending household. Female migrant remittances, like those of male migrants, play an important role in household livelihoods, contributing to poverty reduction and providing a vital social safety net for many families. To households which send migrants, women's economic migration is no less significant than male economic migration in terms of the role of remittances in securing basic household livelihoods. This is particularly true in the case of Lesotho, since female migrant households appear to be poorer and so many female migrants come from female-centred households. The survey results also reveal a significant number of female-headed households, or households without any adult male members. Given that so many female migrants come from female-centred households, with no husband or male partner, women's migration is especially significant to such households as the primary – often only – source of household income.

The fact that male and female migrant-sending households in Zimbabwe show such consistently similar patterns suggests that the motives for migration from that country are common to the country's population as a whole, across classes and genders. Migration from Zimbabwe, whether by men or women, provides a hedge against the country's explosive rate of inflation and collapsing currency. It assists male and female migrant-sending households to maintain a reasonable standard of living, continue to pay rent and utility bills and purchase basic household goods at ever-increasing prices, through what is to be hoped is a short-term political and economic crisis. Migration from Zimbabwe, it might be argued, is conjunctural rather than structural.[32]

Migration from Lesotho seems to be more a response to entrenched household poverty, especially acute in female migrant-sending households, and to the lack of alternative local employment or livelihood options. Male and female migrant remittances provide the main or even sole source of household livelihood, although female migrant-sending households, many of which are female-centred, remain significantly deprived of basic needs. Migration is seen as economically necessary and can be said to be structural rather than conjunctural.

Male migration from Swaziland resembles that from Lesotho, being largely a response to long-term household poverty. Male migrants' remittances act to alleviate poverty and reduce deprivation from basic household needs. The motives for Swazi women's migration are rather less obvious, given female migrant-sending households' relatively higher socio-economic status. However, women from Swaziland who migrate for purposes of work are doing so partly in order to meet the costs of treating their family members' health problems, possibly related to HIV-AIDS. The epidemic can scarcely be described as conjunctural, especially in this region, but for individual families, it might indeed be the event that precipitates a decline in a household's economic fortunes, and thus acts as a spur to migration. Of course the lack of local professional opportunities for qualified women, and the better prospects of employment in South Africa, may also be a large part of the explanation.

Motives for Mozambican men's and women's migration are more difficult to hypothesise, given the inconsistent gender patterns in the data, but household poverty and deprivation are clearly strong push factors for both male and female migration and migrant remittances act as important alleviators of poverty to those households that receive them. Overall, the data shows that cross-border migration - while fulfilling slightly different roles in different countries and in some cases on the basis of gender - has both real and perceived positive economic impacts on households in Southern Africa, where structural poverty is so prevalent and conjunctural poverty both widespread and frequent.

It is the similarities between male and female migrants in terms of the impact of their remittances, despite differences in the demographics of male and female migrants, that are the most striking and most significant. In highlighting these gender-based similarities (and some differences), the MARS data points to possible changes in the nature of men's and women's migration behaviour over the past decade.

Women migrants of the late 1990s were found to be older, more educated, and more likely to be married than male migrants.[33] The MARS data suggest that today's migrant women are becoming younger and are less likely to be married than their male counterparts. It may, therefore, be that differences between male and female migration, and between male and female migrants, are starting to diminish. Certainly young, unmarried women appear to be engaging in 'economic' migration more than they did previously, while male migration is extending into broader spheres of economic activity, both formal and informal, as well as into older age cohorts.

Is it possible that a 'migration transition' is occurring, with mobility increasing (a) for male heads of household in the middle-aged cohorts, and (b) in younger age cohorts, for unmarried single women? Are young migrant women today filling the same role as young migrant men have traditionally done, except that they are better educated and not tied to mine labour? Is staying single, getting an education, and engaging in migrant livelihoods seen as more rewarding for women than getting married and staying home?

At the same time, is male migration becoming more like the 'old' female migration, being practised by older, married heads of household as either a primary or supplementary source of livelihood across a range of occupations and activities? Women heads of household have long engaged in migration as a source of livelihood, but has there also perhaps been an increase in the number of female-centred or female-headed households? If true, this might signal a fundamental social shift in the institutions of marriage and the family.

There does appear to be greater social acceptance of women's migration. Both male and female migration are regarded by migrant-sending households as having generally positive impacts. Gender similarity in the perceived impacts of migration differs from the findings of SAMP surveys done in the 1990s which suggested that women's migration was perceived more negatively than men's migration, e.g., in terms of its social impact on the family. Women's migration for economic purposes thus appears to be becoming more socially acceptable, perhaps as it becomes more necessary and widespread. Female migration is profoundly changing the social landscape of Southern Africa, for if the patterns and trends identified here are both valid and sustained, women's cross-border migration in the region looks set to increase in extent and socio-economic significance.

ENDNOTES

1   S. Chant, ed., *Gender and Migration in Developing Countries* (London: Belhaven, 1992); K. Willis and B. Yeoh, eds., *Gender and Migration* (Cheltenham UK: Edward Elgar, 2000); N. Piper, ed., *New Perspectives on Gender and Migration: Livelihoods, Rights and Entitlements* (London and New York: Routledge, 2007) and M. Schiff, A. Morrison and M. Sjoblom, eds., *The International Migration of Women* (Washington: World Bank, 2007).

2   P. Bonner, "'Desirable or Undesirable Basotho Women?' Liquor, Prostitution and the Migration of Basotho Women to the Rand, 1920-1945" In C. Walker, ed., *Women and Gender in Southern Africa to 1945* (Cape Town: David Philip, 1990); M. Miles, "Missing Women: A Study of Swazi Female Migration to the Witwatersrand 1920-1970" (MA thesis, Queen's University, Kingston, Ontario, 1991); C. Cockerton, "'Running Away' from 'The Land of the Desert': Women's Migration from Colonial Botswana to South Africa, c. 1895-1966" (PhD thesis, Queen's University, Kingston, Ontario, 1995).

3   B. Dodson, *Women on the Move: Gender and Cross-Border Migration to South Africa*, SAMP Migration Policy Series No. 9 (Cape Town, 1998); B. Dodson and J. Crush, "Gender Discrimination in South Africa's 2002 Immigration Act: Masculinizing the Migrant" *Feminist Review* 77 (2004): 96-119; B. Dodson, "Gender, Migration and Livelihoods: Migrant Women in Southern Africa" In Piper, *New Perspectives on Gender and Migration*; T. Ulicki and J. Crush, "Poverty, Gender and Migrancy: Lesotho's Migrant Farmworkers in South Africa" *Development Southern Africa* 24 (2007): 155-72.

4   S. Maimbo and D. Ratha, eds., *Remittances: Development Impact and Future Prospects* (Washington: World Bank, 2005); D. Ratha and W. Shaw, "South-South Migration and Remittances" World Bank Working Paper No. 102, Washington, 2007.

5   J. Crush and D.A. McDonald, eds., *Transnationalism and New African Migration to South Africa* (Toronto: CAAS, 2002).

6   L. Guarnizo, "The Economics of Transnational Living" *International Migration Review* 37 (2003): 666-9.

7   S. Bracking, "Sending Money Home: Are Remittances Always Beneficial to Those Who Stay Behind?" *Journal of International Development* 15 (2003): 633-44; J. Crush and B. Frayne, "The Migration and Development Nexus in Southern Africa: Introduction" *Development Southern Africa* 24 (2007): 1-23; R. Lucas, "Migration and Economic Development in Africa: A Review of the Evidence" *Journal of African Economies* 15 (2007): 337-95.

8   D. Ratha and P. Shaw, "South-South Migration and Remittances" World Bank Working Paper No. 102, World Bank, Washington, 2007.

9   W. Pendleton, J. Crush, E. Campbell, T. Green, H. Simelane, D. Tevera and F. de Vletter, *Migration, Remittances and Development in Southern Africa*, SAMP Migration Policy Series No. 44 (Cape Town, 2006).

10 Pendleton et al., *Migration, Remittances and Development*.

11 Ibid.

12 Ibid., p. 15.

13 Ibid., p. 15.

14 Dodson, *Women on the Move*.

15 With the exception of mine labour, South African immigration and labour policy is still highly restrictive towards the employment of foreigners, especially at the lower end of the skills spectrum. This effectively discriminates against the legal employment of foreign women.

16 Pendleton et al, *Migration, Remittances and Development*.

17 Dodson, *Women on the Move*.

18 J. Crush and J. Gay, "Migration and Remittances in Lesotho: An Overview" Report for INSTRAW, New York, 2008.

19 Dodson, *Women on the Move*.

20 Ibid.

21 Ibid.

22 This pattern has been clearly identified in Lesotho in another study: see C. Boehm, "Fields, Mines and Garments: Production, Social Reproduction and Changing Livelihood Pathways in Lowland Lesotho," PhD Thesis, University of Copenhagen, 2004.

23 D. Tevera and J. Crush, *The New Brain Drain from Zimbabwe*, SAMP Migration Policy Series No. 29 (Cape Town, 2003).

24 D. McDonald and S. Jacobs, *Understanding Press Coverage of Cross-Border Migration in Southern Africa Since 2000*, SAMP Migration Policy Series No. 37 (Cape Town, 2005).

25 The small number of Mozambican households sending only female migrants makes analysis of this sub-sample problematic. While results for Mozambique's female migrant-sending households are included in the remainder of the report, these should only be seen as suggestive.

26 J. Crush, A. Jeeves and D. Yudelman, *South Africa's Labor Empire* (Cape Town: David Philip, 1991); J. Crush, and C. Tshitereke, "Contesting Migrancy: The Foreign Labour Debate in Post-1994 South Africa" *Africa Today* 48 (2001): 49-70.

27 Significant numbers of Zimbabwean nurses are employed in British hospitals and care facilities; J. McGregor, "Joining the BBC (British Bottom Cleaners): Zimbabwean Migrants and the UK Care Industry" *Journal of Ethnic and Migration Studies* 33 (2007): 801-24.

28 Household income and expenditure data should be taken as suggestive rather than in any way definitive, given the difficulties associated with collecting such data in reliable form.

29 The inconsistency between some of these percentages and those recorded in Table 13 (whether migrants send money) is likely caused by the nature of remittances, with more regularised remittances perceived by respondents as

constituting income while once-off, emergency remittances (Table 21) may not have been perceived as such.

30 Table 17 shows the reported average amount of the previous month's expenditure in various categories, using median rather than mean values to provide a more accurate reflection of average expenditure levels, as this reduces the influence of one or two respondent households with high expenditure. Note too that the values in Table 17 are only for those households reporting the particular expenditure (i.e. excluding the 'zero-expenditure' households in each category), and also represent expenditure in a particular single month rather than averaged over a year.

31 Rand is the South African national currency, which is tied to the currency value in Lesotho and Swaziland on a 1:1 basis. For Zimbabwe, precise conversions are impossible, owing not only to the existence of parallel official and unofficial exchange rates, but also to rapid increases in the rate of inflation. Expenditure values should therefore not be used to make inter-country comparisons, although they can still be used as indicators of differences between male and female-migrant households within the Zimbabwe survey sample.

32 This adopts language used by Iliffe to describe different forms of poverty: (a) long-term, entrenched, *structural* poverty, and (b) temporary, contingent, *conjunctural* poverty, such as occurs during a drought; J. Iliffe, *The African Poor: A History* (Cambridge: Cambridge University Press, 1987).

33 Dodson, *Women on the Move*.

MIGRATION POLICY SERIES

1. *Covert Operations: Clandestine Migration, Temporary Work and Immigration Policy in South Africa* (1997) ISBN 1-874864-51-9
2. *Riding the Tiger: Lesotho Miners and Permanent Residence in South Africa* (1997) ISBN 1-874864-52-7
3. *International Migration, Immigrant Entrepreneurs and South Africa's Small Enterprise Economy* (1997) ISBN 1-874864-62-4
4. *Silenced by Nation Building: African Immigrants and Language Policy in the New South Africa* (1998) ISBN 1-874864-64-0
5. *Left Out in the Cold? Housing and Immigration in the New South Africa* (1998) ISBN 1-874864-68-3
6. *Trading Places: Cross-Border Traders and the South African Informal Sector* (1998) ISBN 1-874864-71-3
7. *Challenging Xenophobia: Myth and Realities about Cross-Border Migration in Southern Africa* (1998) ISBN 1-874864-70-5
8. *Sons of Mozambique: Mozambican Miners and Post-Apartheid South Africa* (1998) ISBN 1-874864-78-0
9. *Women on the Move: Gender and Cross-Border Migration to South Africa* (1998) ISBN 1-874864-82-9.
10. *Namibians on South Africa: Attitudes Towards Cross-Border Migration and Immigration Policy* (1998) ISBN 1-874864-84-5.
11. *Building Skills: Cross-Border Migrants and the South African Construction Industry* (1999) ISBN 1-874864-84-5
12. *Immigration & Education: International Students at South African Universities and Technikons* (1999) ISBN 1-874864-89-6
13. *The Lives and Times of African Immigrants in Post-Apartheid South Africa* (1999) ISBN 1-874864-91-8
14. *Still Waiting for the Barbarians: South African Attitudes to Immigrants and Immigration* (1999) ISBN 1-874864-91-8
15. *Undermining Labour: Migrancy and Sub-contracting in the South African Gold Mining Industry* (1999) ISBN 1-874864-91-8
16. *Borderline Farming: Foreign Migrants in South African Commercial Agriculture* (2000) ISBN 1-874864-97-7
17. *Writing Xenophobia: Immigration and the Press in Post-Apartheid South Africa* (2000) ISBN 1-919798-01-3
18. *Losing Our Minds: Skills Migration and the South African Brain Drain* (2000) ISBN 1-919798-03-x
19. *Botswana: Migration Perspectives and Prospects* (2000) ISBN 1-919798-04-8
20. *The Brain Gain: Skilled Migrants and Immigration Policy in Post-Apartheid South Africa* (2000) ISBN 1-919798-14-5
21. *Cross-Border Raiding and Community Conflict in the Lesotho-South African Border Zone* (2001) ISBN 1-919798-16-1

22. *Immigration, Xenophobia and Human Rights in South Africa* (2001)
    ISBN 1-919798-30-7
23. *Gender and the Brain Drain from South Africa* (2001) ISBN 1-919798-35-8
24. *Spaces of Vulnerability: Migration and HIV/AIDS in South Africa* (2002)
    ISBN 1-919798-38-2
25. *Zimbabweans Who Move: Perspectives on International Migration in
    Zimbabwe* (2002) ISBN 1-919798-40-4
26. *The Border Within: The Future of the Lesotho-South African International
    Boundary* (2002) ISBN 1-919798-41-2
27. *Mobile Namibia: Migration Trends and Attitudes* (2002) ISBN 1-919798-44-7
28. *Changing Attitudes to Immigration and Refugee Policy in Botswana* (2003)
    ISBN 1-919798-47-1
29. *The New Brain Drain from Zimbabwe* (2003) ISBN 1-919798-48-X
30. *Regionalizing Xenophobia? Citizen Attitudes to Immigration and Refugee
    Policy in Southern Africa* (2004) ISBN 1-919798-53-6
31. *Migration, Sexuality and HIV/AIDS in Rural South Africa* (2004)
    ISBN 1-919798-63-3
32. *Swaziland Moves: Perceptions and Patterns of Modern Migration* (2004)
    ISBN 1-919798-67-6
33. *HIV/AIDS and Children's Migration in Southern Africa* (2004)
    ISBN 1-919798-70-6
34. *Medical Leave: The Exodus of Health Professionals from Zimbabwe* (2005)
    ISBN 1-919798-74-9
35. *Degrees of Uncertainty: Students and the Brain Drain in Southern Africa*
    (2005) ISBN 1-919798-84-6
36. *Restless Minds: South African Students and the Brain Drain* (2005)
    ISBN 1-919798-82-X
37. *Understanding Press Coverage of Cross-Border Migration in Southern Africa
    since 2000* (2005) ISBN 1-919798-91-9
38. *Northern Gateway: Cross-Border Migration Between Namibia and Angola*
    (2005) ISBN 1-919798-92-7
39. *Early Departures: The Emigration Potential of Zimbabwean Students* (2005)
    ISBN 1-919798-99-4
40. *Migration and Domestic Workers: Worlds of Work, Health and Mobility in
    Johannesburg* (2005) ISBN 1-920118-02-0
41. *The Quality of Migration Services Delivery in South Africa* (2005)
    ISBN 1-920118-03-9
42. *States of Vulnerability: The Future Brain Drain of Talent to South Africa*
    (2006) ISBN 1-920118-07-1
43. *Migration and Development in Mozambique: Poverty, Inequality and Survival*
    (2006) ISBN 1-920118-10-1
44. *Migration, Remittances and Development in Southern Africa* (2006)
    ISBN 1-920118-15-2

45. *Medical Recruiting: The Case of South African Health Care Professionals* (2007) ISBN 1-920118-47-0
46. *Voices From the Margins: Migrant Women's Experiences in Southern Africa* (2007) ISBN 1-920118-50-0
47. *The Haemorrhage of Health Professionals From South Africa: Medical Opinions* (2007) ISBN 978-1-920118-63-1
48. *The Quality of Immigration and Citizenship Services in Namibia* (2008) ISBN 978-1-920118-67-9